Planning, Common Sense, and Superior Performance

Planning, Common Sense, and Superior Performance

by

Erwin Rausch

INFORMATION AGE PUBLISHING, INC.
Charlotte, NC • www.infoagepub.com

Library of Congress Cataloging-in-Publication Data

Rausch, Erwin, 1923-
Planning, common sense, and superior performance / by Erwin Rausch.
p. cm.
Includes bibliographical references.
ISBN-13: 978-1-59311-878-5 (pbk.)
ISBN-13: 978-1-59311-879-2 (hardcover)
1. Decision making. 2. Business planning. I. Title.
HD30.23.R39 2008
658.4–dc22

2007047726

Printed in the United States of America

CONTENTS

PART I

Foundations

PART II

Issues which Managers Should Consider in Every Decision and Plan

---

PREFACE

The other day I went to an early morning meeting, or at least that is what I thought I was doing. It turned out that only one other person showed up. We waited a while and then realized that there had been some misunderstanding and we went back to our offices. When I opened my email, there was a message from Jim, the guy who had called the meeting, telling everyone that he had to postpone it. He offered two alternate dates and asked everyone to let him know which would be OK. The trouble was that he sent that message on the afternoon of the day before the meeting and the two of us did not have a chance to check our email.

Was this an unusual situation? Not really. It happens all the time, with all kinds of things, at work and at home. I am sure that you have had many such instances, where someone did something, probably thoughtlessly, that annoyed, frustrated or otherwise hurt you, even if you can't recall a specific instance right now.

That happened because the person failed to think of all the things that should have been considered.

For years, in my writing and live presentations, I have said that everyone can make better decisions and prepare better plans if a few questions are asked before going ahead—whatever that may be. I did suggest six or eight specific questions but made it clear that users need not accept them but should modify them to make them better fit their specific needs, or to develop their own. The important thing was to develop the habit to think of a useful set of questions with every decision and plan.

No one disagreed, but then I had the feeling that my words had little impact.

Some people thought that I should do research to show that the questions did not come out of thin air.

That always struck me as both frustrating, and also funny.

Planning, Common Sense, and Superior Performance, pages xiii–xv

Why research something that is obvious to everybody? For example, one of the questions I was suggesting was to ask whether there were people who would be unhappy with something that was done, or was not done, when a plan or project was implemented. Like what happened to me when Jim, who called the meeting didn't realize that he had to do more than just send the message—he had to make sure that it was received.

Now, I could research that by asking a thousand people whether it might make sense to ask themselves whether something about a plan they were developing deserved asking about its likely impact on people—and what could be done to avoid or blunt a negative one. I don't think that I would have to keep track of the answers. There is little doubt that the overwhelming majority would agree that such a question, just before going ahead, would not hurt, and might even be a good idea.

With, all but a dozen agreeing, I could then say that this question did not come out of thin air.

Some people would argue that just asking would not be enough. There would be a need to show that better plans would actually result. For that it would be necessary to check whether people asked themselves that question before they implemented their plans—and then to see whether the plans of those who asked the question were "better" than those of people who did not ask it.

Now that raises the question of how they could judge whether the plan was indeed better. Maybe, it would be adequate if they could say "Oh, if I had only thought of so-and-so and done something to avoid such and such a problem." That still might not be adequate and more rigorous evaluation of the outcome of the plan might be necessary.

But why? Doesn't the most fundamental common sense tell us that we sometimes overlook things, maybe unnecessarily, when we make decisions or develop plans?

What are some of the things we overlook? In my opinion, it would be worth giving at least fleeting thought to a set of questions such as:

- Would we benefit from getting input from someone, and whom?
- Are we doing something that will annoy or hurt someone?
- What could we do to make sure we communicate the plan effectively?
- Can we avoid laying the seed for conflict or how will we deal with it effectively, if it is unavoidable.

A few thoughts about benefits from using a set of questions, before we turn to the questions and related matters that are the subjects of this book.

1. Not only will regular use of the questions help you improve plans and decision because you are less likely to overlook something that should be considered, it will also prevent you from

   (a) Jumping to conclusions prematurely
   (b) Acting on the basis of inappropriate assumptions
   (c) Starting implementation in a direction that addresses only some of the challenges and not all

2. When in a meeting, thinking of the questions might lead you to consider and offer relevant thoughts that are not being mentioned by someone else. Would that have a favorable impact on the way you are perceived by those at the meeting?

ACKNOWLEDGMENTS

In light of the three histories, to give full due to all those who have contributed effort, time, thought, and advice, to this volume as well as to the preceding ones, would bring a substantial increase in the size of the book. I have therefore attempted to credit only those who have been of help with this specific volume, and I must ask for understanding from the many others whose contributions to the foundation volumes (Rausch, 1978/1985, Rausch & Washbush, 1998; Carter & Rausch, 1999) are not specifically mentioned here, but can be found in those books.

First I would like to thank Dr. Marcel Fulop and Dr. Thomas Abraham, previous and current chairs of the Management Science Department at Kean University and of the MIS department in the Nathan Weiss Graduate School of Kean University, for giving me the opportunity to teach courses on the 3Cs, (Rausch & Washbush, 1998). These experiences brought awareness that the approach used in this book might make it easier than the previous books, to learn the issues and questions that are most likely to bring high quality management, and leadership-in-management decisions and plans.

Emerald Publishing's Internet presence, (http://www.emeraaldinsight.com) deserves mention here. It leads to a plethora of articles on management, many of which have contributed to my personal development, and thus, indirectly, to this book.

Herbert Sherman, Director of the Division of Business, Southampton College, Long Island University, certainly deserves mention for his many suggestions to, and co-authorship of academic papers on the subject of this book and its predecessors.

Library research is an essential element in all serious writing. Though operating within the confines of the limited resources available in a community library, the help I received at the Cranford Public Library was invaluable. John Malar, the Director of the library sometimes personally

Planning, Common Sense, and Superior Performance, pages xvii–xviii helped me directly. The reference librarians Robert Salmon and Ben Stanley, on whom I called most frequently and whose expertise in finding useful volumes was especially helpful, and Mary C. Skrumovsky who cheerfully helped with some tedious searches, deserve expressions of my gratitude. They were able to access databases and library stacks in collections all over the state. That made searches far easier, and so much less time-consuming than could have been done without their help.

Much credit goes to organizations where I conducted pilot seminars of the new perspective and to the graduate and undergraduate students in my courses at Kean University. They helped me see more clearly how to better present the unfamiliar focus on issues and considerations for decisions and plans, as foundations for effective leadership-in-management actions.

Finally, though obviously not last, I have to thank my wife for the patience with which she has read sections of the manuscript, not once, not twice, but sometimes a number of times, and whose down-to-earth comments were often painful, but unfailingly valuable.

—Erwin Rausch

The author welcomes comments and questions. These should be addressed to

Erwin Rausch
P.O. Box 457
Cranford NJ 07016
USA
E-mail: didacticra@aol.com
Tel: (908) 276-5413

CHAPTER 1

INTRODUCTION

Our common sense often tells us immediately what to do and we do it without much further thought. Sometimes it is only one of the things we consider before going ahead with whatever we plan to do.

It is not adequately appreciated that most decisions are made, and simple plans are arrived at solely by following our common sense, more or less intuitively. Other, more complex plans require a combination of intuitive thinking and a deliberate analytical thought process.

We are only vaguely aware that our common sense is based on what we have learned from experience and even from schooling. We do know, of course, that it is steadily becoming more comprehensive and sophisticated. Just think of how much better your common sense is today than what it was when you were a teenager.

This book is intended to help you enhance your common sense as well as your ability to prepare plans that are most likely to lead to successful outcomes. A big claim, to be certain, but undoubtedly a valid one.

Experience and learning translates into better judgment and reasoning ability. More precisely, new knowledge led to thought habits that became so solid that you spend hardly a moment on decisions and plans to which they apply. That is how common sense and judgment mature.

Practicing the relatively simple formula that this book offers, and developing the habit to apply it regularly, will help you take a quantum step toward a higher level of common sense. At the same time, the book will provide you with tools that will sharpen your ability to develop plans and

Planning, Common Sense, and Superior Performance, pages 1–14

make decisions at work and at home. You will acquire a more comprehensive perspective than you probably have now.

In addition to guiding you toward developing better plans, the book will show you how to be a more effective leader.

A BRIEF SUMMARY OF THE BOOK'S MESSAGE

If you manage anything, with or without staff, are preparing for managerial responsibilities as a college student, or if you seek to take a managerial career track, this book can be of significant use to you. It does not matter whether your career is in business, non-profit organization, or government, in health care, retail, engineering, or transportation, just to name a few. The concept presented here applies to matters that, directly or indirectly, involve people. If you are, or expect to be a manager with a small or a large staff, this book will not only help you develop the managerial aspects of your common sense, it will also help you become a better leader. However, even if you are on a professional track where you manage a function, but do not, or will not have anyone reporting to you, your work still has impact on people. In these professional positions the leadership aspects of your managerial responsibilities may just be of smaller impact, overall, on your work. You will, nevertheless bring better results if you consider many of the thoughts and concepts discussed here.

Moreover, most professionals are frequently in positions on teams or projects where they are likely to assume leadership responsibilities. In these situations, the concepts discussed in this book can also be very useful.

Even where your leadership and management responsibilities, involve family affairs, most of the sections of this book can be valuable. They address key issues important for interpersonal relations, and they do it from a unique and comprehensive perspective.

The book's message is exceedingly simple. It consists of four parts:

1. You can significantly improve your ability to manage, and to lead, if you can apply a very sound approach to all your responsibilities. So far that is obvious.
2. Such an approach will help you steadily enhance your common sense and thus will ensure that will pay attention to all matters that may influence the outcomes of your decisions and plans. That means your common sense should help you to ensure that you are considering all issues relevant to whatever you are doing or planning. This book suggests an approach in the form of a model with eight universally applicable, actionable questions, shown as either primary or secondary, depending on the frequency with which each one may be

relevant to specific situations. For each of the eight questions, subsidiary questions provide more specifics on issues included under the main question. You can use this model (the one suggested in this book and first listed in Chapter 2), adapt it, or use one that is equally comprehensive, valid, universally applicable, and actionable.

3. To make full use of the questions, you have to develop the habits that will help you to apply them effectively. The habits should bring regular consideration of a number of relevant questions, This is by far the most important part of the book's message.
4. To gain the full benefit of the habits you should continue to broaden your knowledge, and related skills, pertaining to the questions and the issues they raise. You can, however, apply the questions immediately, after reading through Chapter 2, with the knowledge you have acquired in your education and work experience. As you use them, you will expand, trim, or change the list until you have one that satisfies your style and needs. When you apply the model presented here, to decisions and plans, you will see more and more of the issues that the questions raise and that you should consider. Addressing these issues is likely to raise your curiosity and thus lead to greater knowledge, and higher and higher levels of quality for your decisions and plans. That will make you, truly, a learning manager/leader who can inspire others to follow your lead. At the same time, this thought process will gradually become part of your intuitive response to the challenges you face.

Does all this mean that you will be more successful immediately, or at least very soon? Not necessarily. There is likely to be improvement that will make you, and the people around you, feel good about the effort you have devoted to items 2 and 3 above. However, beyond that, much depends on all the uncontrollable elements in your situation. Whether those are favorable in a specific situation, or not, the message of this book is likely to be of considerable help. The thought discipline it demands will help you bring the changes that will lead to greater success, whatever that means to you.

You will find that this book is different from other books that cover similar topics. Rather than describing the findings of research on what is, and possibly what should be, it looks at the world from a realistic perspective. It is based on theory and on the research from which theory springs, but when it presents theory it does so with teeth—with direct guides to application. While it is not deliberately inspirational, it does, subtly, send the message that you can reach any realistic goal you set for yourself, provided you persevere in gradually enhancing your decision-making and planning competence. Gradually is the key word. The approach suggested here helps you to develop sound planning habits and enhances your intuitive ability to make sound decisions—your "common sense"—which can greatly reduce the effort and time you need to reach your goals.

In your private life, and at work, the questions bring better decisions. If you are a manager who has a department or an entire organization reporting to you, your use of these questions can serve as a model for your managers and staff members. As a result, all decisions and plans in the areas under your jurisdiction will be made better. There will be more appropriate delegation, goals will be set when desirable, staff members will gain greater competence and find the greatest possible satisfaction, and the highest level of motivation, in their work. In other words, people will achieve more, because they will WANT to strive for greater organizational success.

STRENGTHS AND LIMITATIONS

The book, of course, has both strengths and limitations. To see these in perspective it is necessary to look at the four dimensions of management and leadership competence and to clarify how and where the book helps to sharpen them. These four are:

1. Managers and leaders must be competent in interpersonal skills
2. They have to understand the considerations pertaining to financial issues
3. Most managers and leaders should be competent in a relevant discipline

These first three dimensions are briefly discussed in Chapter 12, under *Other Decision-Making Issues.*

4. Since all actions are based on decisions, the fourth dimension is the most important one. It concerns management and leadership decision-making and planning competencies. that are the primary focus of this book. This dimension covers the issues that everyone should think about when making decisions in a leadership role at work, at home, and in avocational pursuits. These are the issues that will help them be effective leaders, as managers or in other positions, when called on to assume a leadership role. Many of these are described in the original, most widely known description of management functions—the management cycle of planning, organizing, leading (or influencing or directing) and controlling. In addition, some people consider the leadership dimension to include steps pertaining to developing a vision, overcoming resistance to change, ensuring posi-

> tive attitudes including ethics, enhancing creativity, and obtaining buy-in and commitment. The book looks at these in depth but considers leadership and managerial decisions and plans to include even more responsibilities. It covers all decisions that bring about effective control (so the organization will define what it wishes to achieve and organize itself to work toward that end with appropriate participation by all stakeholders), achievement of the required competence, and development and maintenance of a satisfying environment for all stakeholders, especially staff members.
>
> The term leadership will be used here to refer to leadership-in-management, (which involves the non-technical aspects of a leader/manager's work) because there is no one common term that describes them. Leadership best describes the function that involves the issues that affect the work of people in organizations. Here it also is meant to distinguish leadership in all organizations, those that are private for-profit as well as those in public or private non-profit fields, from leadership in the arts, scientific research, many sports, social issues, and even in politics. While there are similarities in personal traits of outstanding leaders in all fields, the skills which made Joan of Arc, Einstein, Mother Theresa, Martin Luther King, Matisse, Pavarotti or Michael Jordan, outstanding leaders in their fields, are strictly related to their science, cause, or art, and are significantly different from those which are needed to be an effective leader in an organization. These leaders are not called on to satisfy the operational responsibilities of managers. At times, one or the other, however, may also have been a leader in an organization, such as leaders in a battle, or in a scientific, artistic, sport, or social action field.

A few more words about two definitions: many people see sharp distinctions between what is meant by *manager* and what is meant by *leader.* Since most managers, to be effective, have to assume leadership roles, the word *manager* will be used to include the manager's leadership function, to avoid repetitive use of the clumsy term *manager/leader.*

It is also important to remember that leadership-in-management decisions and plans should consider three types of issues:

- The technical (or functional)
- The decision making processes and psychological influences
- Those that pertain to leadership[1]

---

1. The word *leadership* will be used here to denote leadership in organizations, without implying position authority, and to distinguish it from leadership in the arts and elsewhere where it would have different meaning.

While the technical issues are beyond the scope of this book because they are different for every field and discipline, the other two types of issues will be discussed extensively in the various chapters.

HOW TO USE THIS BOOK AND FOR WHAT

There are two uses for this book: a) as a text for a course, and b) for self-development.

When used as a text, it might be worthwhile to start with coverage or a brief review of the theories in Chapter 14, as background for the model explained in the book.

For self-development a different approach may be best. Though the book quickly gets to the point in each section, you are not likely to read it straight through. In fact, you would be doing yourself a great disservice if you struggled to finish it in one sitting. You will get more from it if you take it in little bites. It will be useful, however, to glance at the pages on which the eight questions and their subsidiary questions are outlined, before doing extensive reading. (There is a very brief overview in Chapter 2 under D. The Eight-Questions Model); more detailed outlines are in the first few pages of Chapters 3 through 11. These latter twenty pages or so can be identified easily in the Table of Contents. They can help with visualizing the entire model so that other reading has a solid foundation.

Much of what is discussed will take on added meaning when you look at it a second time, or if you continue reading after a few days or even weeks. Because this book is not meant to be devoured in one sitting, some thoughts are repeated, possibly several times. Occasionally this may also be to emphasize the respective thought. Please ignore such repetition if you consider it redundant.

You might ask yourself what you will gain from the effort and time you might devote to reading or studying this book. Even if you will not actually develop the habits recommended here, you will probably think of more issues when you make decisions and prepare plans, than you would have done without this reading. Furthermore you will undoubtedly apply *some* of the concepts discussed here to real decisions at work, in vocational pursuits, in clubs, and in family life. If you do, you are likely to either; pick up the book again and read more, or to expand your knowledge of the issues you have begun to consider, without further reading. In either case, your decisions and plans will be based on sounder foundations than they would have been otherwise. One more benefit that will be pointed out more than once. If you will be familiar with the eight questions, you are likely to notice issues that others will overlook when discussing a decision or plan. Pointing to such issues is likely to enhance your image as a thoughtful person.

THE BOOK'S CONCEPTUAL FOUNDATION[2]

Though it is solidly based on the research and theories reported on in the literature, the process suggested here does not provide specific answers for each aspect of each decision or plan. Furthermore it does not directly address the technical/functional issues. It does, however, use successively more detailed questions which, when considered in a decision, help to ensure that all relevant issues (the non-technical ones, and the technical ones) are given some thought, and that all underlying concepts are considered. The rest is up to the decision-makers/planners and their assessment of the needs of the specific situations or challenges facing them.

As the questions become progressively more specific, they zero in more and more closely on the issues they raise and on the most useful alternative courses of action. For the actual choice of action, the specific facts and technical aspects of the situation must, of course, be taken into account. This means that, even after the questions and the situation have been considered, they do not point to things that should be *done*—merely to matters that should be *considered.* Only after the 8-Questions Model has helped to define what are likely to be the desirable alternatives, can the best one be selected, with appropriate participation, to arrive at what should be *done.*

If you follow the steps suggested here (and thus think of the eight questions) for decisions and plans, you will identify more valuable options (alternatives) and will select a more desirable one, than if you do not use such an approach. (See *Realism and Two Caveats* below.)

Still, do not expect that all decisions and plans will turn out great—outside influences may affect results more than the quality of the decisions (see below). If you apply the concept suggested in this book, your batting average of good and great outcomes is highly likely to improve.

DECISIONS AND PLANS, AND THEIR QUALITY

To be of high quality, a decision or plan has to pay careful attention to detail—to all the relevant issues that should be taken into consideration.

This can be seen when considering the meaning of quality. It is easy to recognize really poor quality. For instance, when an automobile breaks down frequently, we consider it to be of poor quality. Whenever something fails to perform a major function for which it is intended, we recognize that as being less than satisfactory. Lack of quality, then, is relatively easy to see.

2. Please see Sections A and B in the book's Appendix for more detail

High quality could be considered to be the absence of inadequacies, and that is less easy to see. Is a car with a radio that does not work, a car of poor quality? Probably not, but it also is not of high quality—at least not as high as an identical model where the radio works fine.

A decision or plan that was arrived at by considering everything that deserves thought, and where nothing was overlooked, is certainly of higher quality than one that was less carefully considered. Does thoroughness of thought guarantee that the outcome of the decision or plan will fully meet expectations? Of course not. Outcome is too dependent on totally unpredictable external influences. That is why many carelessly made decisions and plans turn out to have great results and some carefully considered ones fall far short of what they were intended to achieve. To measure quality, then, one cannot look at results, but rather at the quality and thoroughness with which all relevant issues were considered in the identification of alternatives and the choice of the preferred one.

That is true for decisions and plans at work, in avocational pursuits, and in private life. It holds in the private and in the public sectors, in manufacturing, extracting, agricultural and service organizations, and in non-profits. Still, very little attention has been devoted to identifying what makes for quality of decisions, and particularly of those decisions that are the foundation of planning, and implementation of plans.

As incredible as it may sound, the literature pertaining to management, leadership, and supervision, does not even contain a comprehensive, organized approach to the subject of managerial decisions. There is a body of knowledge and books on the technical aspects of decision-making and decision analysis, including decision processes (the steps in decision-making (Golub, 1997; Goodwin & Wright, 2004) and mathematical formulae for many of the aspects that can be quantified. There are computer programs called decision support systems, and of course, also books providing guidance to supervisors, on their responsibilities. There is also a literature segment that concentrates on behavioral issues in decision-making such as personality influences, attitudes toward risk, ideas and people, other psychological factors affecting aspects of a desirable outcome, ability to cope with ambiguity, etc. There are also books on errors that affect decisions such as Decision Traps (Russo & Schoemaker, 1989) and others (Heifetz, 2002; Nutt, 2002; Plous, 1993; Russo & Schoemaker, 2002). Because these last issues are tangentially relevant, Decision Traps is briefly discussed in Chapter 14.

Nothing can be found, at this time, which discusses all the issues that managers, as leaders, should consider when making their decisions or preparing plans, whether they manage functions that affect stakeholders, and/or supervise a staff.

This book is intended to help redress the lack of emphasis, in the literature, on the development of a comprehensive approach to issues that should be considered in decisions and plans, as the foundation for all leadership and management action.

Don't expect that all decisions and plans will turn out great—outside influences affect them—but batting average is highly likely to improve

BENEFITS OF USING UNIVERSALLY APPLICABLE QUESTIONS IN DECISIONS AND PLANS

There are several benefits that you will gain if you develop the habit of applying a series of questions to every significant decision you have to make, and to plans you are preparing:

1. *You will make better decisions.* That does not necessarily mean that the outcomes of all your decisions and plans will indeed be better because they often depend on unforeseeable circumstances and on matters completely beyond your control. Over time, however, your batting average of "good" outcomes will certainly be better.
2. *You will enhance your image as a competent person.* If you occasionally ask one or more of the questions that are relevant to a discussion, in a meeting or with individuals—in your own team and in those involving people from other departments or on higher organizational levels, you will be seen as a person with considerable insight and one who can be counted on to make a useful contribution.
3. *You will continue to enhance your competence in decision making and planning* because the questions motivate you to look deeper into the skills and knowledge that can help you apply their conclusions more effectively.
4. *The benefits listed at the end of the Preface,* just prior to Acknowledgments.

A FEW POINTS ABOUT THE USE OF UNIVERSALLY APPLICABLE QUESTIONS IN DECISIONS AND PLANS

Most people have a tendency, when faced with a decision, to immediately either list the alternatives that come to mind, or to go even more directly to a specific solution based on intuitive, common sense reasoning. In situations that present themselves fairly regularly, this approach is usually quite appropriate. In less familiar situations, or in more complex ones, it is useful to look at the eight managerial/leadership questions, that may bring attention to issues of which at least one or two might have been overlooked, but that deserve consideration because they will lead to more thoroughly considered decisions and plans. They are therefore likely to bring more desirable outcomes than decisions made without them. The groups of issues raised by each one of the eight questions, then, since they encompass all the responsibilities of the decision maker, bring closer review from the perspective of a more specific, universally applicable, comprehensive, and actionable, view.

A quick glance at the eight questions, as suggested in this book, or a similarly thorough list, can be a sound step and lead to high quality solutions that reflect all the relevant issues. The Illustrative Example below may show how. It shows the use of the questions to ensure appropriate participation and provides some idea of the subsidiary issues the lie behind one of the eight questions. It gives a clear picture of how issues point to answers (though they do not provide them), or at least to direction on where to find them.

The process also lends itself to learning in levels, with key concepts (the questions themselves) at the first level, during the first 'visit'. Expansions could then be looked at, first at the subsidiary questions on what could be considered, and more detailed issues possibly including those that involve the underlying theories, at later times.

Practicing appropriate participation (with emphasis on 'appropriate') is one of the most important leadership and management responsibilities. In contrast to some of the other questions that may be relevant only occasionally, most of the issues it raises should be considered whenever a decision, or a series of decisions (as in a plan) has to be made. (See Chapter 2 for a complete list of the primary and secondary questions).

The analysis in the example below represents a review of the thought process that should precede action. It does not mean to suggest that action should be taken on all the things that come up. Specific steps that should be implemented depend on the needs of the respective situation.

It might be useful to repeat here that decision makers can gain much of the benefit of the use of this question even if they do not seek out the more detailed issues discussed below, but merely give thought to the respective question—participation in this example—just to the who, how (including on what), when, and where of it, based on their respective knowledge and experience level.

There also can be a different, yet interesting benefit to thinking about the 8 questions in a meeting. Because there is considerable redundancy—thought of many issues are likely to arise when thinking of more than one of the questions—they thus help to ensure that none of the relevant ones are overlooked. As mentioned above, in a meeting, they can help you identify issues that may be overlooked by the other meeting participants.

Your image will undoubtedly be advanced if you can point to such issues occasionally.

AN ILLUSTRATIVE EXAMPLE

As mentioned above, participation in an organization might involve individual or several managerial or non-managerial staff members, and individuals outside the respective team or department. (See Chapter 5).

Four major sets of issues require consideration:

- *Who,* specifically—one or more than one person—should be involved in this decision or plan
- *How*—with what role, and on what aspects of the decision/plan—with little input as would happen if only notified of the decision after it has been made, or the plan was prepared, with a request to cooperate, or with more impact on the decision or some aspect of the plan, up to full authority (power) with minimal input from the manager
- *When*—at the start of the deliberation, or at some later time
- *Where*—in meetings, in individual face-to-face contacts, or in some other medium

Asking just these four questions, based strictly on past experience, is likely to point to thoughts that might otherwise not have been considered. There are detailed issues behind each of the four questions that can be helpful, Whom to involve in a decision or plan, when and with how much of a voice, leads to thoughts about:

- The specific relevant expertise which is needed and which the individuals being considered for participation can bring
- How strongly prospective participants feel that they should be involved
- How well a prospective participant is likely to be able to predict the reaction of one or more groups of stakeholders
- The respective work-maturity[3] of potential participants
- The urgency and importance of the decision(s), etc. (see Chapter 6 for more detail)

It should be clear that rapid consideration of the issues mentioned above point to specific selection of individuals who could or should partici-

3. Work maturity is not a matter of age, but rather the extent to which individual participants, or a group, can be counted on to accept responsibility for their inputs, and for their respective roles in implementation.

pate in a decision or plan, and to how or when they should be asked to participate.

Hopefully this brief example has broadened awareness of the ways in which asking the overall question (who should participate, how and when) draws attention to successively more detailed, relevant issues that can help to bring thoroughly considered decisions and plans. At the same time, thinking of the more specific issues brings reminders of concepts, theories, and research findings that can be used to lend confidence to specific answers. Still, just asking the 'overall' question will ensure that participation is not overlooked in a decision or plan, even if the selection of individuals is done with less care than would be possible with consideration of the subsidiary issues.

The titles of Chapters 4 through 11 point to fairly broad questions (the main questions) that, in turn, remind of some or all of the specific issues that are raised by the subsidiary questions. If they are considered in decisions and plans, the chances are high that they will bring the best possible outcomes.

Giving quick thought to the main questions and the subsidiary ones suggested here, or with a similar, equally universal, comprehensive, and actionable list is obviously a useful habit. It stimulates selection of those, which contain more specific issues that are relevant to the situation, and thereby avoids the high probability that some short-term or long-term aspects of the situation will be overlooked. Leaders, managers and other decision makers will achieve the highest possible levels of success if they develop the habit to quickly review the four primary questions and the four secondary ones to asses which are relevant and then look at the specific issues that the relevant ones raise. They will then better identify the desired outcome conditions, as well as the best alternatives to consider, and select the most desirable one. They will be learning managers who continue to gain deeper insight into the full meaning of the questions. Success is especially likely if they encourage managers reporting to them, and their staff members, to follow their example.

It is easy to come to the conclusion that there often is not enough time to think of a list of responsibilities, questions, or groups of issues, when a decision has to be made. This, too, is at best only partially true. Important decisions, are rarely made quickly and the few minutes that a fairly careful mental review of issues may require, may not add any time at all. If the questions are used, they are well worth the effort to achieve the more comprehensive solutions they are likely to bring. More important, though, even in urgent decisions, highly beneficial results might be derived from the brief moment that a quick run through of all eight main questions would use. That is especially true since most of the time, some and possibly several of the questions can immediately be set aside as not relevant because they have previously been considered and action has been taken to satisfy them.

The human brain is capable of incredible speed once it has trained itself, as research into the uncanny abilities of speed-chess masters has shown, and as is demonstrated in sports, in musical instrument virtuosity, and even in typing. The highly structured approach brought by the habit of assessing which questions are relevant, and then thinking of the specific issues to which they point, allows for surprisingly rapid selection of those which apply. It alerts the decision maker to the situation-relevant ones and to those that, among them, are most likely to add valuable thoughts which an initial intuitive reaction might otherwise have overlooked. Possibly most important, development of the habit of asking questions will gradually bring significant improvement in common sense because the latter is obviously built on successful experience. (As is confirmed by the fact that common sense improves with age—with greater life and professional experience).

One technique that can further help with the development of the habit is the use of key words for each question. Such key words are suggested in the relevant chapters, four through eleven.

REALISM

You might ask yourself what you will gain from the effort and time you might devote to reading or studying this book. Even if you will not actually develop the habits recommended here, you will probably think of more issues when you make decisions or develop plans, than you would have done without this reading. Furthermore you will undoubtedly apply *some* of the concepts discussed here at work, in avocational pursuits, in clubs, and in family life. If you do, you are likely to either pick up the book again and read more, or to expand on the issues you have begun to consider, without further reading. In either case, your decisions and plans will be based on sounder foundations than they would have been otherwise.

TWO CAVEATS

1. The approach suggested here is not the only way to ensure that decisions and plans consider all relevant issues. There are undoubtedly other ways a decision maker can use to help ensure that all managerial responsibilities are covered. One such list can be drawn from the *Handbook of Leadership Development* by the prestigious Center for Creative Leadership (McCauley & Moxley, 1998). It refers to leadership

capacities under four headings: a) Ability to interact socially, b) Creativity, c) Critical Evaluation and systematic thinking, and d) Empowerment. Some of these can be converted to questions. However, they are not as comprehensive and actionable as the ones offered in this book. The latter appear to be more thorough and practical than any other currently described in the literature. Furthermore, as mentioned before, even if you adopt the list of main and subsidiary questions from this book, you should still adapt them to your personal needs, situation and management style.

2. The outcome of a decision or plan often depends heavily on circumstances beyond the control of the decision maker(s) and these often cannot be predicted with any degree of accuracy. Hence, even the poorest decision or plan can result in a most desirable outcome if the circumstances turn fortuitous. The opposite is, of course, also true—the most carefully considered one could bring highly undesirable results if events interfere and nothing can be done to change course. There is considerable discussion in the literature on behavioral aspects of decision making and in the technical discussions of risk, that provide insights into ways for dealing with uncertainty and chance (Goodwin and Wright, 2004; Hoch & Kunreuther, 2001; Plous,1993; Wright, 1985). Exploration of uncertainty and chance are outside the scope of this book since they apply only after all relevant issues have been identified. That is after the application of the eight questions ends and consideration of the specifics of the situation determine the choice of the preferred alternative.

PART I

FOUNDATIONS

CHAPTER 2

USING AN EIGHT-QUESTIONS MODEL FOR BETTER LEADERSHIP DECISIONS AND PLANS

THE TWO TYPES OF ISSUES TO CONSIDER IN DECISIONS AND PLANS

It is not widely recognized that every decision and plan requires attention to two types of issues in addition to the decision-making processes and psychological influences. It is, however, important to distinguish them for a thorough understanding of the limitations of the Eight-Questions Model.

The first type includes issues pertaining to the fairly clearly defined, strictly 'technical' fields, the functional areas, such as the field of work (architecture, engineering, construction, health care, retail, manufacturing, and even psychology, etc.). They also include the functions within an organization such as accounting, marketing, MIS, and many aspects of operations or manufacturing, (i.e. quality assurance and materials process control). Some people speak of these as involving measurements, tools, structures and processes. In all of these there are rather well established criteria that can serve as the basis for decisions/plans. Managers feel more comfortable with these aspects because their education provided guidelines for them, and because early career successes proved their value. These issues, of course, are likely to play more of a dominant role in professional work—in the functional areas mentioned above—than they do in

Planning, Common Sense, and Superior Performance, pages 17–27

the leadership aspects of managerial positions. Functional issues also apply to decisions outside the work environment. Remodeling a kitchen, for instance, requires that technical information about the respective advantages of different types of cabinets or appliances be considered in their selection, as well as the eight questions.

The second type of issues applies to those aspects of decisions and plans that are common to all public and private occupations. They pertain to the leadership-in-management area that was briefly defined in Part B1 of the Introduction and mentioned elsewhere. Assessing decision/plan quality in this area is an entirely different matter, given the lack of criteria and standards. Furthermore, few managers, even those who took management courses during their formal education, received meaningful preparation for these decision issues. In addition to courses in the technical aspects of management, they were exposed primarily to theories with few criteria for applying them in decisions and therefore have far less meaningful guidance than they have in the technical areas. Many if not most managers, and others called on to assume leadership roles on teams or projects, arrived there primarily on the basis of success in their functional specialty. Their decision-making skills are therefore focused on those issues and they pay much less attention to the leadership issues that are emphasized in this book. It is important to realize that, for the leadership aspects of management, in contrast to the functional ones, there are either no universal guidelines for decision and plans available, or only very limited ones, pertaining to specific skills.

Still, it is interesting to note that the ten skills that Whetten and Cameron (1993, 1995), identified in their comprehensive research (see Chapter 14), as most frequently cited by managers, were all non-technical (leadership) skills. All the Leadership Abilities listed in the Center for Creative Leadership Handbook cited previously (McCauley & Moxley, 1998) also are on topics in this 'domain'. None pertain to the functional/technical aspects of managerial decisions. Still, guidelines exist only for specific skills (various aspects of effective communications, conflict resolution, coaching, counseling, etc. With the exception of these guidelines for skills, leadership education is unique in failing to provide guidelines for the decisions on the critical issues that determine quality of leadership.

IMPORTANT DEFINITIONS FOR USE IN THIS BOOK: LEADERSHIP, GOAL, OBJECTIVE, ISSUE, MODEL, KNOWLEDGE, SKILL, COMPETENCY, NORMS, MAIN QUESTION, SUBSIDIARY QUESTION, AND STEPS IN THE DECISION MAKING AND PLANNING PROCESS

The subjects covered in this book have to use words that may have different meaning to the reader than is intended. It is therefore important to clarify the meaning of critical terms, as they will be used in this book.

Leadership denotes leadership in organizations, without implying position authority, and to distinguish it from leadership in the arts and elsewhere where it would have different meaning.

Manager almost always refers to a manager as manager-AND-leader. The cumbersome manager/leader is therefore used only occasionally to remind of this definition of manager

Goal and *objective* are used synonymously even though distinctions are drawn between them in many organizations.

Issue is used primarily to refer to matters that should be considered when a decision is being made or a plan is being prepared. Most of the time, it refers to issues that come to light when one of the eight main questions or one of the subsidiary questions is asked, to provide specifics on the full meaning of the question. Every one of the eight questions, on closer look, leads to several, or possibly even many issues.

Model, though often thought of as a graphic representation of a concept, refers here primarily to the verbal model consisting of the eight main questions, the subsidiary questions that are the core of this book, and the issues to which the questions lead.

Knowledge is used to refer to understanding of a subject, as the foundation for its mental or physical application.

Skill refers to the ability to competently apply the knowledge to achieve a result—either a conclusion or an action.

Competency is intended to include both relevant knowledge AND the skills to apply that knowledge effectively.

Norms refers to the beliefs of people that pertain to the organization's, and their own moral foundation, and appropriate and ethical behavior. These especially involve views on 'right or wrong'.

Main question refers to one of the eight questions of the Eight-Questions Model

Subsidiary question refers to questions that are raised when one of the eight questions is considered in greater detail.

Steps in the decision making and planning process refers to the steps taken for a sound decision that also apply to effective plans, including a) identifying of the desired outcome conditions, b) selection of alternatives, c) the search for useful data/information, d) evaluation of the alternatives, e) selection of the most desirable one, f) implementation, and g) monitoring progress toward the desired outcome. It is important to recognize that all these steps are entirely independent of the 8-Questions model discussed below. However, the eight questions can help to make each of the steps more effective.

DERIVING USEFUL QUESTIONS FOR DECISIONS AND PLANS FROM THE LEADERSHIP-IN-MANAGEMENT RESPONSIBILITIES

The model described in this book is intended to provide quality criteria for decisions and plans. It is derived from a leader/manager's many responsibilities that help to ensure that managerial and non-managerial staff members:

- Are clearly aware of their respective individual roles
- Strive to improve the way they perform their responsibilities
- Receive the support and training they need so they will be most creative and effective, and
- Gain the greatest possible satisfaction from their work

The responsibilities also include ensuring that all staff members:

- Know their jobs
- Are competent for achieving what they are expected to achieve
- Devote the necessary effort to their work
- Get all the information they need and should receive
- Receive both positive and corrective feedback
- Receive support when they need it
- Are aware that the people to whom they report appreciate their contributions
- Are aware that their performance is evaluated factually and fairly
- Can express thoughts and ideas freely
- Are aware that advancement and developmental opportunities are granted on the basis of merit as much as possible
- Etc.

These responsibilities translate into questions and groups of issues pertaining to the questions. Not all the questions deserve consideration for a specific decision or plan. Managers should therefore assess the questions for relevance in every decision. If relevant, they should then be included in the thinking which leads to the determination of all the desirable outcome conditions, as well as to the identification of alternatives and selection of the most desirable one. While emphasizing the leadership issues, some of which managers sometimes overlook, the questions help to ensure consideration of the functional/technical ones, and they point to the need to look at both short-term and long-term implications at all times. They can thus form the foundation for high quality overall decision and plan quality. Possibly most important, they prevent the natural inclination to focus on the more familiar technical/functional aspects, and thus help to ensure that the non-technical issues receive appropriate consideration.

The two types of issues (those pertaining to leadership/management and the functional/technical ones) are automatically integrated by considering topic expertise in the selection of decision and planning participants (those who have the technical expertise) and when goals and tasks are set (since most pertain to technical issues). Applying those questions that are relevant to a specific decision or plan allows fairly objective, and fairly thorough evaluation of quality. The emphasis is on relevance to the specific decision or plan, because, while all questions and the groups of issues to which they lead, should be assessed for relevance, only the applicable ones deserve consideration—the others can be ignored, after a brief, possibly instantaneous evaluation of relevance.

The eight questions help to ensure that all leadership and managerial responsibilities receive the attention that they deserve. Please note, as mentioned in Chapter 1 and elsewhere because it is so important, the eight questions and their specific issues refer to thoughts that should be assessed and considered. They do *not* point to what should be done. The assessment and the questions are universal to all decisions and plans- what should be done is specific to each situation.

To better appreciate the role of the 8-Questions Model, (or of another equally valid list of questions and issues) it is useful to realize that the questions play a role in most of the steps of the entire decision-making and planning process mentioned above. That process is discussed in more detail in Chapters 3 and 12 and in the appendix to Chapter 11. It starts with a) defining the desired outcome of the decision or of a series of decisions such as may be needed for a plan. From there it proceeds to b) the identification of alternatives, c) the gathering of data that is needed to evaluate the alternatives, d) the evaluation itself, e) the selection of the most promising alternative, to f) implementation, and finally to g) constant monitoring to determine whether the desired outcome will be reached and, from there, to decisions on corrective steps if obstacles arose. The process is rarely a straight-line one. Instead, new information or insights that are gained in the steps often suggest revisiting and revising an earlier one. Throughout this process that does not necessarily demand the use of all the questions below, they can, however, add depth without demanding significantly more time for the deliberations.

There is still another aspect to the use of the Eight-Questions Model. Thinking of it also stimulates identification of the less obvious short-term and long-term challenges inherent in the situation, which might otherwise be ignored. The process is thus likely to lead to identification of all the challenges in a situation that deserve consideration, not only the obvious ones.

The objectivity and comprehensiveness of a process that uses a thorough list of issues grouped behind major questions, is based on the extensive theoretical and practical knowledge behind each one of them. It should be emphasized, again, that the four primary and four secondary questions that are discussed here, represent only one way to look at managerial responsibilities. As mentioned earlier, they are not the only way to ensure that decisions and plans consider all relevant issues. There are undoubtedly other models that can be used to ensure that all responsibilities are covered. However, as also mentioned before, the questions and their issue groups listed here appear to be the most comprehensive, universally applicable and actionable list currently in the literature, if it is not the only one. Furthermore it has been stated previously and will be stated in other places: even if you adopt the list of questions and issues from this book, you should still adapt them to your personal needs, situation and management style.

THE EIGHT-QUESTIONS MODEL

The eight questions that are based on the leadership-in-management responsibilities, and on the leadership and motivation theories, are listed below in the order in which they are discussed in this book and with additional brief statements expanding on their meaning. Some are labeled primary because they are likely to be relevant for almost every decision and plan. The others, the secondary ones, may be relevant for many decisions and plans, but usually not for as many as the primary ones. It is useful to think of them by their key words since that requires less memorizing, and then build from there, possibly with reference to their full 'titles' as stated here.

Communications

Question 1—Communications—what could or should be done, if anything, to ensure that everyone is aware of what should be communicated by whom, to

whom, when, and how, so all will have the information they need and can expect to receive? (A primary question)

This question raises issues pertaining to 360 degree, two-way open communications with those who need to know and/or have a right to expect that they be told. It also covers critical communications concepts such as the knowledge, skills, and abilities (KSAs) for effective communications, including the conduct of effective meetings, writing and speaking, listening, probing, communicating with non-verbals (non-vocals), and seeking and providing feedback. It sets the stage for meaningful participation of other people in the decision-making process.

Participation

Question 2—What could or should be done, if anything, so that appropriate participation is used in all decisions and plans? (A primary question)

This question raises issues pertaining to whom the decision maker should invite to participate (staff members and possibly other stakeholders, individually and in groups), in what segment of a decision or plan (some aspects or all), how (from no voice to full authority to make a specific decision), when, and also where. It discusses influences of the characteristics of the situation and of the individuals who could be considered.

Competence, Learning, and Selection

Question 3—What could or should be done, if anything, to achieve the highest possible competence for every action (A primary question)

This question concerns issues about a) who should be selected for teams, projects, or open positions, so most effective use is made of competence strengths, and b) identification of the competence deficiencies that need to be addressed with management of learning, coaching and on-the-job training (OJT). In addition it discusses skills for achieving high level managerial and staff competence.

Satisfaction

Question 4—What could or should be done, if anything, so that stakeholders can gain the highest possible level of satisfaction from the contemplated actions? (A primary question)

Ways to counteract the many negative experiences that each day brings, and avoiding excessive stress, are the primary issues behind this question. Emphasis is on ways to counteract the negatives with pleasant moments for staff members and other stakeholders, to create a satisfying climate for maximum positive (self-)motivation. Semi-tangible as well as tangible rewards are also issues to consider. The purpose in raising this question is to help ensure that internal and external stakeholders (including staff) will be as satisfied as possible, or at least not so dissatisfied that problems will ensue.

Progress and Performance Reviews

Question 5—What could or should be done, if anything, so that greatest benefits can be derived from progress and performance reviews, and performance evaluations? (A secondary question)

This question reminds of the functions of progress and performance reviews, and their relationship to organizational justice and performance evaluations. Underlying issues concern what can be done to gain the greatest benefit from performance evaluations.

Coordination, Cooperation and Conflict

Question 6, What could or should to be done, if anything, to assure the highest possible level of coordination and cooperation? (A secondary question)

This question addresses the role of procedures in coordination and the broad requirements for full cooperation with people and with procedures. It emphasizes the need for special attention to the impact of change and to the anticipation or settlement of potentially harmful conflict/disputes that may bring obstacles to effective cooperation.

Norms, Organizational Justice, Ethics, Positive Discipline, and Counseling

Question 7—What could or should be done, if anything, to stimulate or maintain appropriate norms, organizational justice, ethical policies/behavior, positive discipline, and competent counseling? (A secondary question)

This question helps to ensure that issues pertaining to norms (including those on diversity and conflicting values), organizational justice, ethics, and positive discipline, as well as the role of a leader/manager in counseling on work and personal problems, and on career decisions, are considered, when relevant.

Goals and Action Steps

Question 8, Goals and/or action steps—What, if anything, could or should be done about possible use of goals to achieve the desired outcome? (A secondary question)

This question is applicable only if an organization either uses formal goals or plans to use them. The question explores issues pertaining to setting of goals that may be needed to achieve the desired outcome, such as whether a goal or goals should be set, what makes for a high quality goal, and what related matters should be considered if goals are to be used so they will bring all their potential benefits.

If an organization does not use goals, formally, it is likely to prepare plans for achieving the desired outcome conditions. In a way, what is to be accomplished with such plans is essentially the same as one or more goals. However, only some of the issues of the formal goals process would apply.

Though not a pronounceable acronym, *CPCSPCNG*, is a word that consists of the first letter of the key words above. It can be useful when developing the habit to think of all eight questions.

To visualize these eight questions in a diagram one could think of the words 'Decision or Plan' at the top level of a four level structure. The first two questions (Communications and Participation) would be on the next level because they apply to all decisions; the next two (Competence and Satisfaction) would occupy the third level because they are important, and otherwise often overlooked; they should usually be the first things to consider with communications and participation. The final and lowest level would contain the remaining four questions (Coordination/Cooperation, Norms, Reviews, and Goals when applicable) that are listed as secondary questions.

Managers/leaders will consider both, the technical/functional and leadership-in-management issues if they develop the habit to briefly assess the components of the four primary questions, and the four secondary ones or similarly useful questions or issues, for relevance to the specific situation. That assessment will happen almost instantaneously once the habit has become part of the decision makers' intuitive reasoning. The leadership-in-management issues are inherent in all questions and the technical issues, when they are not immediately apparent to the practitioner, are brought to mind when considering what goals or plans to set, and in selecting participants with expertise that may be needed to make a high quality decision or plan. It is likely that few issues, if any, will be overlooked because there is considerable overlap between the issues that lie behind the questions. Usually more than one question will remind of any one issue.

Important note: The first time someone makes a decision or prepares a plan with the use of the eight questions, or a similarly useful list, requires that all questions are first briefly reviewed and assessed for relevance with respect to that decision/plan. Later decisions may not require an equally detailed review, at least for a while. Some of the secondary questions, and even some aspects of primary ones, fade in importance because they concern matters that, once considered, might not have to be given careful thought for some time. For instance, once issues pertaining to work norms and ethics, selection, training, manager competence in using appropriate participation, tangible rewards, etc. were reviewed, and action was taken or was not needed, these issues may not be relevant to decisions or plans in the near future. Questions pertaining to communications, participation and satisfaction, however, are almost always relevant. Those questions and issues which will have faded from relevance should probably be touched on with at least a fleeting thought, so it will be apparent when they have again become relevant, or possibly are relevant from a different perspective. Also, the development of habits does not lend itself well to picking and choosing. It may therefore be best to run through all questions with the incredible speed of which the mind is capable.

A reminder is probably appropriate here: Please note that, as mentioned in Chapter 1, and above in this chapter, the eight questions point to what thoughts should be assessed and should be considered. They do *not* point to what should be done. The assessment and the questions are universal to all decisions and plans; what should be done is specific to each situation.

DECISION AND PLAN QUALITY MONITORING, WITH AND WITHOUT TECHNOLOGY

As complex as it may seem, monitoring the application of the Eight-Questions Model in decisions and plans, to ensure high quality is really quite easy.

In manual or spreadsheet mode, managers could maintain records of the application of the questions in a simple table with the numbers or key words of the questions heading the vertical columns, and the specific decisions/plans being made on the horizontal rows. Entering a few key words about the latter, and checkmarks in the columns, would take less than a minute each time. Still, the record would not only show what issues were considered, but also help to strengthen the habit to think of them. At the same time, the record would stimulate further learning by encouraging reflection on what was done well and what might have been overlooked—especially when the outcomes were disappointing.

In computerized mode, the program could not only record but also analyze each decision and plan. The foundation for such an analysis lies in the extensive literature in the behavioral sciences (the literature on motivation, especially). Specific data that is relevant to an individual organization does not have to be established in advance since the program could also adapt itself (in crude artificial intelligence mode) more and more to the specific situation of the organization. It could build and draw on a constantly self-updating database that could include relevant characteristics of staff members called on for participation. For the latest research findings, the computer program could update from a university-based server (or be manually updated) to take new research on any of the underlying concepts into consideration. Such computerized monitoring would bring even more benefits than a manual system.

CHAPTER 3

APPLYING THE EIGHT-QUESTIONS MODEL

A Basic Analysis Example

The decision-making process that will be used to analyze the example situation in this chapter, builds on the brief outline of the steps in the process, in Chapter 2, early in Section C, just before the listing of the eight questions, and on the discussion in the segment on decision-making in Chapter12. Extending the process with the eight questions can make decisions easier and will, most likely, bring better outcomes. A hypothetical but realistic scenario will be used as an example in this chapter for an abbreviated illustration of the application of the questions—which will be discussed in greater detail in Chapters 4 through 11.

In this chapter, the analysis is rather basic, assuming that most readers have only limited knowledge of the leadership-in-management issues as presented in this book. In an appendix to Chapter 11, more detail will be provided in a second analysis of the same scenario. There the analysis will be done the way a manager with more knowledge of the Eight-Questions Model might make it. Then, Chapter 13 discusses a more comprehensive example to further illustrate the use of the model.

Planning, Common Sense, and Superior Performance, pages 29–44

THE EXAMPLE SCENARIO

A high tech company used a very nice telephone recording when answering calls to the Help Desk. It expressed empathy with the person who is holding on the line. However, traffic on the line had become very heavy and some customers had to hold on for more than 25 minutes. Meanwhile the recording repeated, very frequently, how much the tech support people understand the situation and explained that a representative will soon pick up, that they are doing their best to get to the customer quickly and that, when that happens the customer will get the same high quality service as the person being helped at the moment. It even told some customers, from time to time, that they were next, even though that did not seem to be true at all times.

The recording and the program supporting it, which had been intended to improve customer relations, understandably began to have a negative impact when more and more customers reached the frustration stage. As the complaints increased, John, the Vice President of Sales and Marketing became aware of them and started to work on the problem. Reporting to the Vice President are the Director of Marketing and the Director of Sales. To the Director of Marketing reports a Customer Service Manager who is responsible for customer relations. The person in charge of the telephone system is the Director of IS/IT who reports directly to the President because that position is also involved in product development. A Help Desk supervisor who reports to IS/IT is in charge of the team of staff members who answer the telephone.

ANALYSIS PROCEDURE (INTRODUCTION)

To analyze this, or any other situation, the steps outlined in Section C. Procedure Steps, below, can be used. Like the list of eight questions, these steps are not the only way to proceed. However, they have been shown to lead to comprehensive high quality decisions and plans, and they are likely to uncover short-term and long-term challenges that deserve consideration but are not immediately apparent. In this or any other hypothetical situation, the analysis does *not* result in recommendation of any specific actions that should be taken. In a real situation, it does lead to identification of the features of comprehensive alternatives from which the best one can then be selected. However, only someone in the situation itself, who will know enough about the specifics of the relationships and the history of previous events that might affect the current situation, can go beyond analyzing what actions *could* be considered. Deciding on the specific actions comes *after* the analysis has been completed; it requires detailed knowledge of the situation. For effective implementation, in addition to competent analysis, the relevant technical/functional and interpersonal skills are, of course, needed.

It is important to see clearly that the analysis merely represents the kind (the type) of thinking that should precede action. It does not mean to imply that action should be taken on all the things that come up in the thought process. Which of the conclusions from the analysis should be acted on, always depends on the specific situation. In other words, the analysis points to what should be *considered*, and *not* to what should be *done*.

It is also important to realize that the detailed, and seemingly lengthy analysis presented here, takes very little time (and may even use less time, overall, since most decisions do require some analysis). When the time to correct errors or inadequacies is considered, the time for using the questions may actually be less than traditional approaches for experienced managers—those who develop the habit to think of the Eight-Questions Model when making decisions and preparing plans. Even in highly complex situations, the process described below is likely to either use less time, overall, or add only a few minutes, at most . Furthermore, the analysis here assumes that it is the *first* time that the company uses the thorough procedure involving the Eight-Questions Model. As previously pointed out, future use of the model by managers in the company could still use the same process but some of questions may not be relevant for some time, because they have been resolved in earlier cases. For instance, in the sample scenario, if it were decided that all managers should enhance their project management skills, then the issue of managerial project management competence might not arise until a year or more later, were it to become apparent that a refresher might be desirable.

Finally it is useful to see that, if *every* individual with managerial responsibilities uses a set of questions such as the one described here, then challenges will be met *best* at *every* level of the organization. Goals (formal or informal) or plans will be most appropriate for the situation, policies and procedures will be aligned, and there will be the highest possible cooperation—as well as coordinated attention to all aspects of decisions that cut across departmental lines. When higher-level managers use this process, they become role models, and coaches, who guide the managers reporting to them and/or members of their staffs to become capable of accepting delegation effectively, and to use questions for enhancing the quality of their decisions and plans. In the most effective organizations, managers delegate extensively, and they are visible by 'walking around' so they are available to managerial and non-managerial staff members (directly reporting to them) who need help/support or coaching with one or the other aspect of a delegated responsibility.

One More Note: If a manager does not use a comprehensive set of questions with every significant decision, as few managers do, the world does not collapse, of course. Some managers even make fairly good decisions/plans, frequently, without awareness of the benefits of such an approach. However, their performance will not match what it would be, if they did use a thorough, integrated set of questions, based on *all* their responsibilities.

PROCEDURE STEPS

The following decision-making procedure steps consider the fact that most decisions present more facets than are immediately apparent. An analysis of the situation follows the listing of the steps. Please note that these procedure steps would apply to all decisions and even to most plans. The relationship of these *steps* to the *eight questions* is important to keep in mind. The steps are just what they are called—steps in the decision-making process. The eight questions are used to make the steps more effective—primarily Steps 1, 2, 3, 4, 6, and possibly even 7. (This list states the steps a little differently than they were presented previously—primarily by including the use of the 8 questions—Steps 2 and 3.):

1. *Preliminary* identification of the elements of a desirable outcome, one that would solve the respective problem, face the challenge, or address the opportunity. (Kepner & Tregoe, 1965, 1981)[1]
2. Review of each one of the four primary and the four secondary questions to identify those that may be relevant to the situation—'pruning' the list by removing from consideration those questions that are

1. When identifying the desirable outcome elements, and deciding on plans (or goal areas and specific goals), there are five groups of issues to consider; the first one is not brought up directly but emerges in participation (and also in goal setting). The others are the topics of four of the eight questions that are often given inadequate emphasis:
   - The technical/functional issues
   - The communications needs of the situation
   - Issues to ensure that the necessary and desirable competencies will be available where needed
   - Issues related to ensuring that stakeholder satisfaction will be as high as possible, but definitely not so low as to create obstacles
   - Issues related to appropriate participation

   Most people can easily identify many of the technical/functional things that should be considered for action. It is the other three, the communications, competence and satisfaction issues that are often either neglected or ignored. *A major benefit of the use of a comprehensive sound model, such as the Eight-Questions Model, is to help decision makers and planners think of these latter issues and give them equal attention so the process will be more comprehensive and thus of higher quality, at least from the leadership perspective.*

not needed in the specific analysis. At the same time this review may reveal elements that might be useful to add to the desired outcome conditions.

3. Review of each one of the relevant questions in any order (participation and communications would always be relevant) to help identify what should be considered in the other steps in the decision making process. Please note that these questions help to make each one of the steps more effective by bringing attention to issues affecting the step that might otherwise be overlooked.
4. Identification of alternatives to achieve the desired outcome. Here the questions help to ensure that no desirable aspect of each one of the alternatives is overlooked.
5. Collection of any information that is not yet available but might be needed or desirable. With that information, additional alternatives, and possibly also changes to the desired outcome conditions may become apparent, or existing ones be revised.
6. Evaluation of the alternative plans resulting from the preceding steps in preparation for selecting the preferred one. This step applies the information (factual data), that may be available from Step 5, possibly with the use of decision support systems, as well as the 'common sense (intuitive or emotional inputs) of the decision maker(s) or planner(s), and the reversibility[2] concept, in the evaluation. The preferred alternative should satisfy all aspects of the relevant questions which deserve some form of action, and, of course, also the desired outcome conditions. Here, too, the eight questions have similar use as in Step 4. Like Step 2, this step may reveal matters that might be worth adding to the desired outcome
7. Review and possibly revision of the elements of a desirable outcome, and selection of the most desirable alternative (its components).
8. Implementation of the various aspects of the decision or plan, monitoring to see whether they will, indeed, bring the desired outcome, and new decisions if obstacles have developed.

---

2. "reversibility" refers to the possibility of stopping implementation of an alternative without any, or very little penalty or cost, and proceeding with another alternative that will then appear more desirable in light of the experience with the one that will be reversed.

THE ANALYSIS

This analysis is from the perspective of the Vice President of Sales and Marketing, as it might be made by someone who is aware of the Eight-Questions Model and the decision-making steps but does not have detailed knowledge of their meaning. It follows the decision-making steps outlined above but, in this chapter, it proceeds only through Step 3. What someone not directly involved in the situation can say about the other steps is discussed in the expansion of the analysis in the appendix to Chapter 11.

The issues discussed in each question might be raised by the VP or by other managers involved in the respective relevant discussions.

To get the most benefit from this analysis, it might be useful for you to think how you would approach the challenge in the scenario, if you were the VP, before you read on or, with respect to each question (and Step 1.) before the discussion presented here.

Step 1

Preliminary identification of the elements of a desirable outcome (to result from the decision/plan). It might be useful here to again point to the importance of defining these *before* starting the other steps in the analysis. Desirable outcome conditions are a snap-shot of the situation as it would be if they were achieved. They provide foundation for looking at all eight questions, and especially for deciding on plans (or any goals) that may be most appropriate.

Desirable outcome conditions, that might be identified during initial planning meetings include:

- (a) Revised tape message and program that overcome the problem with the existing one
- (b) Faster tech support response
- (c) Optimum staffing level
- (d) High level competence of help-desk staff and manager
- (e) At least adequate satisfaction of all stakeholders (staff, customers, suppliers, other departments, etc.)
- (f) Ensuring adequate communication of decisions and steps to all those who should be kept informed.

It should be noted here that, in addition to the use of appropriate participation in the process, communications, competence, and satisfaction, are the primary purely non-technical (leadership) aspects of the desirable outcome. The other elements involve technical issues at least as much as non-technical ones. Since even relatively unsophisticated managers with less than average leadership competence are likely to identify a, b, and c, as desired outcome elements, it is attention to d, e, and f, that distinguishes the more competent from the others. It is worthwhile to remember that communications, competence, and satisfaction, should always be considered when deciding on the desirable outcome conditions.

Step 2

Review of the eight questions (not necessarily in the order presented below, but *in any order*) to identify those that may be fully/somewhat/possibly relevant to the situation:

- Key word: *communications* always relevant
- Key word: *participation* always relevant
- Key words: *competence, learning, and selection* always relevant
- Key word: *satisfaction* always relevant
- Key words: *progress and performance reviews* somewhat relevant
- Key words: *coordination, cooperation and conflict* relevant
- Key words: *norms, ethics, etc.* somewhat relevant
- Key words: *goals/plans* relevant

Strictly speaking, all eight questions could be relevant (only, of course, if they were not acted on as a result of the analysis of a previous challenge, possibly by another manager, and do not need to be revisited).

Step 3

Review of each one of the *relevant* questions in any convenient order to identify what insights they may bring, including possible revision of the desired outcome conditions. To reinforce what has been said above: this review is based, in part on the detailed discussion of the eight groups of issues in chapters 4–11. To avoid unnecessary complexity at this stage, the review does not reflect much of the detail in those chapters, but looks at the issues the way an experienced manager might, who has not previously seen them in the context in which they are presented here.

Before reading the analysis below, if you are really interested in this approach, it might be worthwhile to read the pages in this book where the specific questions are discussed (see beginnings of Chapters 4–11).

Communications

Here the issues deserving consideration pertain to what to communicate, by and to whom (360 degrees), when, and how, up and down, between staff members, managers, departments, etc., through channels or direct as appropriate, one-way or open two-way. This means that John, the VP, should consider communications, including those pertaining to:

- Informing customers of the efforts to provide better help line service,
- keeping other teams and departments informed on matters where coordination and cooperation may be needed
- keeping staff and other stakeholders informed of any plans that might affect them and that they should be aware of
- other matters potentially of interest to staff members and other stakeholders
- issues pertaining to manager and staff competence analysis and development with respect to communications

Further analyzing one of these groups of issues, as for example 'keeping other teams and departments informed on matters where coordination and cooperation may be needed' would show that the issues involve informing staff members, and especially those on the Help Desk, of progress on almost all aspects of the plans, direct or through channels, possibly with ccs to higher management levels when appropriate. Some messages might be purely informational; others might contain requests for comments and/or suggestions from a few or all these staffers. Who should send the verbal, written, or electronic messages is another issue to be addressed, as well as the questions that pertain to the route of such communications—direct between staff members or through channels.

John could, for instance, in initial meetings or in individual contacts, with the Directors reporting to him, and any others such as the IS/IT Director, discuss these communications needs as part of the identification of alternative plans for achieving the desired outcome. With respect to these issues he would seek a consensus of what should be done so that all managers and even key staff members would be aware of them. The discussion would, of course, include steps to ensure that the department managers would monitor implementation. They might include approaches to help ensure that communications, as much as possible, are not one-way sharing of information, but two-way communications that would bring feedback, whenever appropriate.

As in all of the other eight questions, if formal goals are used, they may emerge for some or all of these communications issues and, conversely, the goals may trigger thought of further desirable communications actions. If goals are not used, these issues should be considered in the plans.

It is useful to see that the selection of topics to communicate (the 'what' of communications) is often largely a matter that involves the technical aspects of a decision/plan, while the by whom, to whom, when, and how, involves non-technical considerations at least as much as technical ones.

Participation (On What, by Whom, How, When and Where)

Participation refers to the ways in which managers at all levels, and staff members, select others to share in decisions and in development of plans. These others could be staff members, managers reporting to them, or they could be people at all levels in other departments, where there is expertise that might be needed, or from whom cooperation is desired.

For instance, in the identification of alternative plans to consider, for reaching all the desired outcome conditions, John might involve the other Vice Presidents and possibly also the Directors involved with the projects. For deciding on alternatives for plans in the departments, appropriate participation requires that all those who will have implementation responsibilities are represented. For specifics with respect to preparation of a revised tape message and the accompanying program, John might ask the Director of Marketing to proceed with the project in coordination with the Director of IS/IT, requesting progress reports from time to time, possibly only after submittal and approval of a plan. The Director of Marketing, in turn might decide jointly with the Director of IS/IT whom to involve in deciding on plans and tasks (or goals) that are to be assigned to the various departments and teams. That would undoubtedly involve the Customer Service Manager, Help Desk Manager and a manager in IS/IT. These managers, in addition to participating in development of the plans (or deciding on goals) would then involve people reporting to them, as desirable, to ensure adequate technical competence and need for appropriate communications. Please note that there is participation at every level—primarily of people reporting to the respective manager, but also of people from other departments where coordination is essential and where, therefore, their views should be sought.

Specific tasks (or goals) for the teams and individuals would be decided on with participation by the people most affected, and with those who have primary responsibility for the remaining desired outcome conditions as well as for the other projects that the analysis of the situation would suggest. It is important to see here that, in effect, the VP has delegated these matters to other managers. Thereafter the VP's role is primarily confined to providing any support they may need.

It is even more important to recognize that selection of the various departments to become involved is based primarily on technical (functional) considerations (the organization's structure). From the perspective of the non-technical aspects of the participation decisions, what is important to see is that every manager involves (selects for participation) members of the respective staff and possibly people from other departments who can contribute valuable insights. Such selection is based on the issues (subsidiary questions) discussed in Chapter 5—the need for technical expertise, the sensitivity to the reaction of stakeholders to the decision/plan, and the work-maturity of the participant(s).

Competence, Learning, and Selection

1. Competence and Learning. Many issues pertaining to competence and learning might deserve consideration in this scenario. These, too, might be discussed in the identification of alternative courses of action, at all levels. Some include what tech support staff members have to learn to provide better service without additional support until new procedures are put in place, and learning that would be necessary to develop competence with implementing new procedures. As mentioned under coordination and cooperation, below, thought might be given to segregate the help desk staff into specialists; that would bring the need for more intensive training in the respective programs. If this is the first time the comprehensive procedure of the Eight-Questions Model is used, identification of opportunities for stimulating motivation for self-development might deserve consideration.

Other learning issues could involve preparation and review of competence profiles for managers and staff members, and preparation of learning plans where there are shortcomings. Serious thought about competence might lead to even deeper issues such as the competence of managers in decision-making, planning, and project management, so that fiascos such as the tech support answering tape would not occur in the future. As in the other questions, if goals are used by the organization, the possible need for setting goals would deserve a closer look.

Finally, again only if this is the first use of the Eight-Questions Model, it might be useful to give thought to competence of managers in working with a set of questions for use in decisions and plans, such as the eight questions in this book or others that are more appropriate for the company, and to training of all staff members with non-supervisory managerial responsibilities in the application of the questions to their needs.

2. Selection. Questions related to policies and procedures for selecting current or new employees for special projects and/or teams, may deserve thought, maybe not in the initial consideration of the possible alternative plans, but certainly prior to implementation. This might apply to selection for the teams that will develop the new recording and the computer program and would be especially important if there have been problems with such selection in the past. Related issues involve the criteria for selection of help desk staff for specialist assignments, and for part-time staff for peak demand periods, should either approach be used for solving the problem.

Selection also provides an opportunity to enhance competence by taking advantage of the competence strengths of staff members when assigning them to projects (see Question 3.3).

Satisfaction

1. Psychological Rewards. The scenario description is silent on the issues related to the quality and quantity of psychological rewards that managers provide for staff members. It would appear obvious, however, that the issues deserve consideration to ensure that staff members gain the greatest possible satisfaction from their work, and that they cooperate enthusiastically with any changes intended to make tech support more useful to customers.

Once thought is given to psychological rewards for tech support staff, the question of the adequacy of such rewards for members of other departments is likely to arise as well as the specific issue of competence development of managers in this vital, yet frequently neglected function. This question provides an excellent example, why an analysis of a hypothetical case cannot determine whether a specific question is relevant. If steps have been taken previously to ensure that managers are competent and effective in using psychological rewards, then this question is not relevant with respect to a situation.

2. Stress. Work-related stress is an important contributor to, or distracter, from satisfaction. In light of the time pressure in tech support, and the customer complaints, it is likely that staff members are subject to considerable work-related stress. Further sources of stress are in the changes that the new procedures will bring. Ways to reduce such stress to reasonable limits present challenges that could be addressed by managers at all levels.

It is worthwhile to note that additional training in how to handle difficult customers might be of help here and therefore could be considered. This thought about stress, and the preceding one on psychological rewards, brought attention to possible learning needs. It also shows how the overlap between the eight questions helps to ensure that nothing is overlooked that might bring short-term or long-term benefits.

3. Other Considerations. In addition to the psychological rewards described above, it is desirable to consider the other expectations of staff members that may require attention to all eight questions. See Question 5.3.

4. Semi-Tangible and Tangible Rewards. There is little that is specific in the description of the scenario that clearly indicates the need to consider issues pertaining to semi-tangible and tangible rewards. Still, tangible incentives, such as bonuses based on performance may be worthwhile to consider, if they are not already in place. These could be in conjunction with the effort to increase productivity of tech support. There are a number of issues that would raise, including determination of the form such incentives should take, their level, and possible requests from other departments for similar opportunities.

In most situations, other than those that specifically concern compensation issues, this topic is not likely to be considered relevant.

5. Satisfaction of Stakeholders Other Than Staff Members. Relations with stakeholders—customers, possibly other departments, shareholders and other investors in the case of the scenario, involve primarily communications issues. With respect to customers it might be worthwhile to lay plans for measuring their satisfaction with whatever changes will be made. To support staff member needs for job security, it might also be worthwhile to take steps to assure them that the company is doing all it can to prevent further company image and sales erosion. Subsidiary issues might pertain to what messages should be sent to outside stakeholders, how they should be delivered, and to ensuring that such communications are coordinated with actions that support them. Again it is worthwhile to note the reinforcement that the satisfaction question provides for the communications question.

Progress and Performance Reviews

There is nothing in the description of the scenario about the way progress or performance reviews are conducted. However, such reviews could, of course, be considered in conjunction with any procedure changes. Some thought on when and how progress on new procedures should be reviewed would therefore seem desirable. Here too, thinking about progress and/or performance reviews might trigger awareness of any inadequacies in the company's process for conducting these, as well as in the performance appraisal policies and procedures. For the distinctions between these, see Chapter 8.

Coordination, Cooperation, and Conflict

There could be many issues deserving attention in this question because extensive revisions of procedures and work assignment are significant changes. They affect staff member reactions and thus coordination and cooperation with people, as well as with the procedures. At the same time, how to prevent or blunt potentially damaging conflicts/disputes deserve thought. Asking this question might be indicated if staffing levels are to be as low as possible. Complete redesigns of work flow in the department that could enhance coordination may deserve consideration, including possibly the creation of specialists on various products who would be more efficient in providing customers with the help they request. (Specialization would ensure that no staff member would have to be knowledgeable in too big a field). Any major change would raise the question about what procedures need to be established and communicated. Alternative media channels might also be worth considering such as a website help service, including easy access to frequently asked questions, fax-on-demand, e-mail, possibly others that new technologies would make available. Procedures for monitoring the effect of such changes might be needed.

Cooperation challenges resulting from conflict/dispute prevention/resolution issues, including training, may also have to be considered if there is reason to anticipate cooperation problems between people or with new procedures.

Norms, Ethics, Positive Discipline, Counseling

The scenario description does not mention anything that might indicate needs in this question. However, being short, the description of the situation does not paint a complete picture. There could well be something deserving further thought. Few organizations have developed an effective positive discipline climate. Many managers are not sensitive to the tacit norms and ethical principles that guide the thoughts and actions of their people, or their perceptions of the justice and fairness in decisions affecting them. Few managers are highly skilled in communicating the organization's norms and ethical principles verbally and through example. Many are not experienced in identifying opportunities for, and conducting counseling sessions. Some of these issues might deserve further thought and inclusion of appropriate steps in plans or, if the organization has a formal goals program, setting of goals for meeting them might be desirable. More effort may be needed to identify and work on inappropriate norms and unethical views held by staff members, and to ensure that managers are competent in doing that.

If tangible incentives were to be considered for tech support staff,—a thought that is triggered by the question on tangible rewards (see above), then that would impact on positive discipline and on perceptions of justice, and thus might present additional issues to consider.

Goals and Plans

The first question pertaining to plans and goals concerns, of course, what the overall goal of the decision or plan should be (what is to be accomplished)—what the desired outcome conditions should be. That question was resolved in Step 1, above. Then, if the organization uses a formal goal system, or is starting one, the question should be raised, whether a goal or goals should be set, with respect to each one of the specific items in the desired outcome conditions. If that question is answered affirmatively, it is necessary to ask what goals might be appropriate. Goals apply to the highest level manager, the Vice President in the example scenario, and also to every manager who is involved with one of the projects generated by the effort to achieve the desired outcome conditions. Most importantly, goals are also for individual staff members who may be asked to accept one or more that will help to achieve a team or department goal. The request to work on a goal has to be made with appropriate participation, of course. Rarely will a staff member object to such delegation, except possibly in instances when the manager is not aware of a competence deficiency or of an already very heavy workload. It is also useful to keep in mind that the goals to achieve a desired outcome help to define it more specifically, even if they are not set formally, and that usually more than one goal is needed to achieve a desired outcome condition.

In the scenario the technical/functional areas immediately apparent for possible goals or actions appropriate for the respective teams, and/or for individuals, might be on:

- Preparation and approval of a script, for a satisfactory tape message
- Preparation of a computer program for implementing the message so it will give accurate information to callers
- Recording of the tape message and testing it in conjunction with the program
- Determination and implementation of optimum staffing for the faster tech support response including evaluation of feasibility of flexible staffing, possibly with use of some part-time employees and/or staff members from other departments, during peak demand periods
- Investigation of possible use of specialized teams
- Analysis of staff and manager competence strengths and deficiencies
- What should be done, if anything to enhance staff and manager competence
- Identification of possible programs to ensure satisfaction of staff and other stakeholders
- What should be communicated to the various departments of the company and when.

It is useful to see that, what is to be achieved by a majority of goals, (or elements of a plan), is often largely a matter involving the technical (functional) aspects of a decision. However, those goals that concern results to be achieved with respect to communications, competence, satisfaction and the other issues pertaining to the eight questions are, of course, leadership aspects of the desired outcome.

Please note: Some people find it useful to ask 'who, what, how, and when' to help them identify issues deserving consideration with respect to each one of the eight questions. Also please note that the analysis *did not* make any specific recommendations on *what to do.* It merely pointed to ideas to *consider* which then lead to specific actions by the people in the respective situation.

As mentioned earlier in this chapter, issues pertaining to decision-making steps 4 through 8 will be discussed in the appendix to Chapter 11—at least the little that can be said about these steps in an analysis of a *hypothetical* scenario where additional information that may be necessary for these steps cannot be obtained.

CONCLUDING THOUGHTS

At this point it may seem as though this analysis process is too cumbersome to conduct with all, and even with important decisions. As has already been pointed out, that is not the case, however, for three reasons: a) once the habit to ask the questions and to evaluate relevance has been established, the thought process occurs with great speed (as speed-chess masters, pianists, and even typing has demonstrated); b) in a real situation, as distinct from a hypothetical one, there is a history which indicates that several, and possibly most of the issues that the questions raise have been resolved in prior decisions or plans and need not be addressed again—possibly making only a few questions relevant; c) in some instances, since fewer matters will be overlooked, errors can be avoided, thus eliminating the need for corrective steps that could possibly take considerable time; d) most important, though, even in urgent cases, a quick run through of all eight main questions might bring highly beneficial results. That is especially true since the structure provided by the eight questions may often bring faster analysis of the situation than a careful traditional one.

Steps that might be considered to effectively address all issues depend, of course, on the specific situation. Concepts, techniques, and even theories that can be helpful when deciding on exactly what to do are discussed in chapters 4 through 12, and 14. As the analysis of the scenario has shown, issues that deserve thought might come up in the review of more than one of the questions. That is part of the beauty of this approach—it has built in redundancy to help ensure that the decision or plan will indeed be of high quality by considering *all* aspects of the situation and not only the apparent ones. Still, despite this redundancy, no more time is likely to be needed for the analysis.

Practice with using this approach—to think of a set of questions, those suggested here or those from another equally sound, universally applicable, comprehensive and actionable list—will develop the habit to use them regularly when appropriate. The habit, in turn, will make the process easy and rapid.

Most importantly, the scenario analysis has shown how more relevant issues will be considered than are likely without the use of this type of approach. A manager who has not developed the habit to use a comprehensive set of questions, would probably not address all of the matters covered by the goals and actions considered above. That manager would recognize and consider most functional aspects but might be less thorough with respect to the non-functional issues such as those pertaining to communications, participation, goals, satisfaction, competence, etc. At one extreme, such a manager might arrange only for the revision of the tape. However, it is also likely that those matters that were not addressed will surface in some other form at some later date. They would then be likely to require more time to correct, and possibly create crises that could have been avoided.

It is probably useful to point out here that it would have been necessary to think of the guidelines several times during the incident, and afterwards, to come up with the thoughts discussed above. That is because the scenario described a large number of decisions. Though the guidelines should be considered several times, only very few are likely to be relevant after the first review. Still, there is benefit to giving fleeting thought to guidelines that are not relevant to the situation itself—they may trigger useful thoughts of matters to consider after the challenge or problem has been resolved.

If you did an analysis yourself before, or while reading the one above—did you consider all the issues or did the slightly greater depth of the analysis above expose some that you would have overlooked?

PART II

ISSUES WHICH MANAGERS SHOULD CONSIDER IN EVERY DECISION AND PLAN

CHAPTER 4

QUESTION 1: COMMUNICATIONS

What could or should be considered, if anything, to ensure that everyone is aware of what should be communicated by whom, to whom, when, and how, so all will have the information they need and can expect to receive?

(Question 1—A primary question)

INTRODUCTION

Appropriately thorough communications should, first of all, be 360 degree—down, up and sideways—in all directions—between levels, between departments, and between individuals. etc., through channels or direct as appropriate. All staff members should be aware of their communications responsibilities as it pertains to their daily routine work and with respect to projects and goals. Communications, especially open, two-way communications is the lubricant for implementation of plans and for all the issues involved in the eight questions.

The organizations should, therefore, ensure that all staff members achieve high level competence in communications-related implementation skills, especially in appreciating the importance of effective listening, probing, and feedback. All managers in an organization need to be aware of their responsibility in that respect.

The information that should be communicated is all the information, irrespective of its origin, that individuals need, that might be useful to them, and often even that they could expect to receive so they would feel

Planning, Common Sense, and Superior Performance, pages 47–53

that they are fully part of the organization. Effective implementation of all decisions and plans, is totally dependent on communications.

The *what,* by *whom,* to *whom, when,* and *how* issues are the specific sub-questions here. Very little can be said about these in a general way since they depend greatly on the specific situation.

There are undoubtedly readers of this book who might want to know why the two remaining "W" questions —*Where* and *Why*—are not also addressed here. The reason is that there are hardly any issues to consider with respect to *Where* except that verbal communications should always consider the location where they take place—the surroundings, the people other than the intended receivers who might be listening, etc. Even less can be said about *Why* to communicate, except that, to obtain the benefits of open communications, it is necessary that as much as possible be communicated to all those who should know or can expect to be informed. For more information about the impact of communications on staff satisfaction, please see the list of staff member expectations in Question 4.3.

Question 1.1

What to communicate depends on the situation, of course, but also involves the appropriateness of the message. As a general guideline, everything that is needed by individuals so they can do their work, coordinate and cooperate with others and with procedures should be communicated. Serious consideration should also be given to communicate what people (stakeholders) expect and/or want to be informed on.

Information that may have a negative impact on the receiver (such as threatening information, but also unsubstantiated rumors) must be considered carefully. It may be inappropriate to transmit such information at the specific time, or even at any time. It also may deserve very careful preparation, and possibly review by management before it is communicated.

Question 1.2

Who should communicate? is directly related to the 360 degrees referred to in the first sentence of this chapter. It should be obvious that, if all staff members and other stakeholders will receive all the information they need or that would be useful to them, the information would originate from all those who have such information. Communicating is the responsibility of managers at all levels and also of all staff members. However, in many situations, when a staff member communicates matters of concern or interest to others, procedures may require that it be done through the manager, and it is the manager's responsibility to ensure that these matters are indeed transmitted. Communications responsibilities, as mentioned above should, therefore, be clearly understood by all. That might make it desirable to include reminders of communications procedures and responsibilities in staff meetings, from time to time.

Question 1.3

To *whom* to communicate? is another consideration that deserves thought. In general, anything affecting an individual should be communicated to her or him, as well as information that the respective person would expect and be entitled to receive, or even would like to receive. There is, however, sensitive information that may have to be kept confidential and to which only selected individuals can be given access.

Question 1.4

When to communicate? also depends on the situation, but there is a general rule that should be considered with each message: the sooner the better. There may be good reasons for not communicating a message at an early time, but many managers tend to hold back desired or useful information longer than is best for the satisfaction of the receivers, and is best for the climate of the organization. Some do so deliberately, but most do so by default—because they are not aware of the possible detrimental repercussions (unintended side-effects) in mutual trust, in perceptions of organizational justice, and potentially also in operational matters.

Question 1.5

How to communicate? involves the question of whether the communication is to be strictly a one-way message, or whether it should be open, two-way, requesting comments, feedback, or suggestions. In addition it involves a) in what medium (individually face-to-face, in meetings or to groups, verbally, in writing, or on some form of electronic medium the communications should take place; and b) whether it is to be through the manager(s). All of these choices obviously involve considerations that also depend on the situation.

Beyond the five subsidiary questions in this communications group, there are important communications skills needed. These include the basic skills of:

- Listening, including empathy and attention to non-vocal/non-verbal messages
- Probing with open and closed questions, and with moments of silence,
- Providing and obtaining feedback, and
- Writing

as well as their application to interviewing, coaching and counseling, showing appreciation, etc.

The only communications skills that will be discussed in this chapter pertain to meetings. The other specific knowledge and skills mentioned above, though critical to effective communications are beyond the scope of this book. There is a vast literature on communications skills that can be used to help managers and staff members enhance their communications competencies. As far as this book is concerned, the emphasis is on issues to consider with respect to communications and a discussion of specific skills topics would lead to far away from this purpose.

Still, it is useful to note that effective verbal communications, but also some aspects of written communications, are much more likely to achieve thorough transmission of messages if all parties to a communication practice effective *listening* and *probing*, and *seeking* as well as *providing*, at least adequate *feedback*. These are the three essentials for two-way open communications in which the sender's message is received, interpreted, and understood as intended.

CONDUCT OF EFFECTIVE MEETINGS

First, two tongue-in-cheek thoughts:

Tongue-in-Cheek Thought 1:

Are you lonely? Work on your own? Hate making decisions?
Hold a meeting.
You Can:

- *See* people
- *Draw* flowchart
- *Feel* important
- *Impress* your colleagues
- *Drink* coffee and *eat* donuts
- *All* on company time

"*Meetings*...the practical alternative to work"—Anonymous

Tongue-in-cheek thought 2—Rausch's Laws of Meetings:

- More meetings are held than are needed
- Most meetings take longer than necessary to bring the desired result
- More people are asked to attend most meetings than are needed
- Few meetings are adequately prepared

The following seven thoughts pertaining to meetings can avoid most of the problems with meetings, including the dissatisfaction of participants who are frustrated by a waste of their time.

1. Maybe a Meeting is Not Necessary

If something can be addressed without a meeting, don't call a meeting, but handle it in an alternate way, by phone, via electronic means (e-mail, the local network or other electronic connection), with memos, etc. Participation does *not* require face-to-face discussion. Often matters that were once considered to require a meeting can be handled with alternate media. The points below, which pertain to preparation, are even more applicable in such a virtual meeting.

2. Prepare Carefully

An agenda is certainly desirable for every meeting and it should be distributed prior to the meeting. If complex decisions or plans have to be made, it is usually more efficient, and satisfying to participants, if they do not have to start defining alternatives. It may be better to present one or two alternatives, and ask the participants to add to them, to revise them, and to choose the best one. Sometimes very useful new alternatives emerge, brought by the more focused thought that the prepared ones stimulated. This approach may avoid some potential conflicts/disputes and the possibility that participants go off in many different directions, including some that may not be really relevant to the decision(s) or plan(s) to be made.

3. Call Only the Necessary People to the Meeting Who Are Really Needed

Often, if not usually, fewer people are necessary to satisfy the technical and acceptance requirements, and relevant items from *other elements of the situation.* (See the issues addressed by Question 2.5 in Chapter 5, and also the section on technical and acceptance quality in Question 2.1) It may be adequate to obtain comments from some people via e-mail, fax, or telephone, before or after the meeting, instead of asking them to attend.

4. Send Timely Notices and Reminders

Whenever possible, notices of meetings should be sent at least two or three days prior to the meeting date and reminders should be sent on the day before the meeting. (See the situation described at the beginning of the Preface.)

5. Urgent Meetings Do Not Necessarily Have to Be Postponed

It *may* not be necessary to postpone an urgent meeting because a critical person is unavailable—especially if it is difficult to get everyone together soon. In these situations it may be possible to consult with that person before the meeting, after it, or possibly even while the meeting is in progress, and make whatever adjustments may come from such a contact. Everyone affected could then be briefed. Occasionally it may be possible and desirable to call a follow-up meeting, but that meeting is likely to be short. In the meantime, useful implementation steps can proceed.

6. State the Objective of the Meeting at the Beginning, and Then Keep the Meeting Focused on That Outcome (Rausch, 1969 and 1971)

Don't allow yourself to get sidetracked. Deal effectively with difficult people. (Bramson, 1981)

7. Conclude with a Plan

Make sure that, at the conclusion of the meeting, there is as clear a plan as possible for proceeding. At that time, all participants should understand the plan. Each person who walks away with an assignment should know it and, as much as possible, should have accepted it willingly. It is often advisable to send a written summary (electronically or otherwise) to all participants, as a record, and to confirm the assignments.

In meetings, as well as in one-on-one communications, it is important to keep listening, feedback, and probing, constantly in mind.

SUMMARY

Communications questions and issues pertain to the what, by whom, to whom, when, and how. They have to be considered with most, and probably with all decisions and plans. Therefore, managers/leaders should, keep their own roles in the communications process in mind. They should also see to it (as mentioned in the Introduction), that everything reasonable is done to ensure that all staff members achieve high level competence in the related implementation skills, especially in appreciating the importance of effective listening, probing, and feedback.

CHAPTER 5

QUESTION 2: PARTICIPATION

What could or should be done, if anything, so that appropriate participation is used in all decisions and plans?

(Question 2—A primary question)

INTRODUCTION AND BENEFITS OF APPROPRIATE PARTICIPATION

It's not my place to run the train, the whistle I can't blow,
It's not my place to say how far the train's allowed to go.
It's not my place to shoot off steam, or even clang the bell,
But let the bloody thing jump the track, and see who catches hell.

—Anonymous

It is impossible to overstate the importance of appropriate participation, when discussing leadership-in-management decision. A good case can be made for the admonition that the first thing that a manager or other professional should consider with every decision and plan, is whom to involve and how (with how much authority for the decision or plan). One form of extensive participation is delegation since it concerns the transfer of part, or all, of the responsibility for making relevant decisions or plans to one or more members of the reporting managerial and/or non-managerial staff. (See Chapter 11, Delegation, Goals, and Participation).

Planning, Common Sense, and Superior Performance, pages 55–64

It should be obvious that participation brings many benefits. It helps to ensure that:

- The best available expertise (possibly including outsiders) is available to address the needs of the plan, project, challenge, problem, or opportunity
- More than one mind reviews the needs of the situation so that most, if not all, relevant technical and acceptance quality issues are considered
- There is appropriate communications
- The many rewarding aspects for participants are gained, especially matters pertaining to satisfaction of participants

It is this last item that can easily be seen out of perspective or even ignored. Sometimes, when a potential participant's ideas may not be welcome, that person may not be consulted even if that may offend her or him and thus bring negative repercussions. This situation was demonstrated by a humorous incident when the question was raised in a class of adults, whether they would consult their mother-in-law when contemplating renovating their kitchen. One student immediately responded with "Over my dead body!" bringing roaring laughter from the other members of the class. It is only when she realized that she did not have to accept any suggestions that she became aware that, not giving the mother-in-law the courtesy of discussing the project, could hurt family relationships. The incident illustrated the need for considering the benefits of participation, which can help avoid inappropriate immediate emotional reactions.

Appropriate participation, then, applies at all levels. At lower levels, it should be used on matters pertaining to the work of the organizational unit and of individual members. Thus, managers should always use appropriate participation by involving managerial or non-managerial staff members directly reporting to them, and those from other departments with whom coordination is important.

Participation can take place in meetings with one person or more than one, and sometimes even without face-to-face contacts. In many instances, comments via e-mail or telephone, or in written messages, before or after the meeting as indicated by the situation, may be adequate or even preferable (see Chapter 4, Conduct of Effective Meetings).

Issues which make participation appropriate include allowing the right amount of authority—sharing of power—not too much, not too little, with the right people, at the right time, on specific segments of a decision or plan (on some aspects or all), using the most appropriate medium or location, etc.

It is useful to appreciate the extent to which appropriate participation (including deliberate delegation of authority/power) can actually help a manager achieve better, rather than reduced ability to manage/lead the respective function or organizational unit. Staff members, individually or in teams, are given the opportunity to provide input, especially when they have relevant technical expertise. Experienced and competent staff members are given wider scope in affecting the decision or plan than those who are new or less competent. For participation to be fully appropriate the manager clearly identifies and communicates the limits of authority for staff members. That is the way the manager retains the critical element of control in the respective situation.

Practicing appropriate participation is likely to lead to higher levels of competence and performance, and greater work satisfaction for staff members. Still, it is important to appreciate that no one can select the most appropriate participation all the time. Over the long run, it is the batting average that counts—the proportion of instances when participation is appropriate or at least perceived so.

Please note that, even if not specifically mentioned here, the words 'staff member' always refer to managerial *and* non-managerial staff members, within the department and in other departments, who should participate in a specific instance.

It is often difficult to see whether or not a manager practices appropriate participation. Take the example of a fire. The battalion chief arrives first, moments before the first two fire engines. He already knows who they are from his two-way radio contacts. The building is heavily involved, with fire pouring out of windows on the first and second floors. Two people are framed in third floor windows, screaming for help. On the radio the chief gives these orders to the two officers on the way with their teams: "John, there are two people on the third floor. Do not hook up (the water hoses). Get these people out." Then he continues: "Bill, hook up and protect John."

Was this participative decision making or was it a set of autocratic orders from a "boss"?

Even though the example refers to a crisis situation where most people would consider "orders" to be appropriate, it could be either, depending on the relationship. If John heard that he has to get these people out or there will be unpleasant consequences, or, if either man felt that the assignment should have been reversed, and they were reluctant to point that out, then there was little or no participation.

On the other hand, it is possible that John interpreted the message as: "Do your best to rescue these people, I know the task couldn't be in better hands." Furthermore, if both knew that, even though this was a crisis situation, they could make a quick plea for changing, even reversing the assignments, and be given full consideration of their point of view, then this was highly participative decision making, displaying very strong mutual trust.

Participation, then, is like a book—it can't be judged by the cover, or, like beauty, can be skin deep, but usually isn't. The mutual trust that is built by many instances of *appropriate* participation is the key to this most important management/leadership action.

SUBSIDIARY QUESTIONS FOR PARTICIPATION

Since participation is not a *yes* or *no* issue, the following questions that make participation appropriate, will be briefly discussed in this chapter. (For a brief overview of major theories on which they are based, see Chapter 14). The questions concern the *who, on what, how, when,* and *where,* of participation in any one specific decision, plan, or group of decisions.

The question that managers should ask themselves, before proceeding with implementation, concerns the type and level of participation by others that will bring the highest level of success.

The overall issue of participation, and most of the questions in this chapter, cover a range. Overall participation ranges from little to extensive participation. Similar to the way mathematicians consider a continuum of numbers, with 0 as the lowest of all the real numbers, so no participation at all is part of the range and can be appropriate under certain circumstances. At this extreme, the manager makes the decision(s) and does not even tell anyone about it. To use a rare example, a manager planning to leave the organization may not want anyone to participate in that decision. At the other extreme, on many projects, competent staff members may be given full authority to make all relevant decisions and to take all appropriate steps on their own.

The specific questions also cover continuums. More guidance, on which point in the respective continuum might be best, is provided by the discussion of the questions below. They affect the selection of the most advantageous point on each of these continuums.

Question 2.1—*Who* Should be Invited to Participate?

Who should participate depends on the expertise required for a high quality decision/plan, both the technical knowledge and knowledge, or sensitivity, to the way the various stakeholders are likely to react to the decision. It also depends on the work maturity of the prospective participant(s). (See Questions 2.1a and 2.1b below).

Question 2.1a—What are the Technical and Acceptance Requirements?

Relevant technical knowledge and expertise is needed for the technical requirement of a high quality decision or plan. Knowledge of how people (all stakeholders, staff and other) are likely to feel about, and will react, is the acceptance requirement. Selection of the best alternative requires as much knowledge as possible for both of these for successful implementation. Therefore (whether the manager or other person responsible to achieve the results, arranges for limited or extensive involvement of other people), the necessary technical expertise has to be available, as well as a reasonably accurate prediction of the likely reaction of the various groups of stakeholders.

The need to ensure that the technical expertise and the knowledge of staff and other stakeholder reactions are available, determines to some extent the specific person or persons who should be consulted or be involved in other ways. Frequently the person with primary responsibility for the plan, project, or decision, may be able to competently supply both these inputs. In those situations, it may be appropriate for participation to consist only of informing all stakeholders in a timely manner. However, especially in important decisions and plans, it may be wise to involve at least one other person with whom to compare views on the technical aspects (with someone who has extensive relevant technical knowledge) and on the likely stakeholder reactions (with someone who has good sensitivity to the views of relevant stakeholders).

It should be noted that there is a connection here between technical/functional and leadership-in-management issues. As was pointed out before, the habit of thinking of a set of questions with every decision, will automatically consider both, those which apply to the occupation and field/discipline in which the organization operates and those which apply everywhere—the leadership-in-management considerations.

The technical and acceptance requirements were illustrated by Norman R. Maier of the University of Michigan in a grid with four spaces (quadrants) (Maier, 1967):

- Low acceptance requirement/low technical requirement
- High acceptance requirement/low technical requirement
- Low acceptance requirement/high technical requirement, and
- High acceptance requirement/high technical requirement.

Two important points about the Maier concept:

1. Acceptance requirement does not refer solely to staff members. If an alternative will impact on other stakeholders such as customers, other departments, suppliers, neighbors, etc., thought has to be given to the issues that would affect their acceptance, and what the implications of rejection by any one group of stakeholders would mean. Sometimes consultation with representative members of these other stakeholders may be advisable.

2. Technical requirement need not be considered as restricted to functional expertise. The conclusions of the diagram could also apply if the technical requirement were interpreted to include understanding the norms of staff members such as their beliefs, ethics, and values (see Chapter 10).

Low acceptance requirement/low technical requirement situations generally involve matters on which nobody really cares what will be done. Everybody wishes that somebody else would make the necessary decision(s) and go on with the business at hand. There are, however, not too many situations of this type in the work environment. A manager who does not see to it that decisions in this quadrant is made quickly, either by assigning it to someone or by making it, gives the impression of a procrastinator.

Matters with high acceptance requirement/low technical requirement, might concern plans to reduce absenteeism or increase attention to certain specific quality details, reduction of waste, better customer greetings, etc. Most matters involving a significant amount of effort or attention by staff members would be in this area, except for those that, in addition to acceptance, require high technical knowledge. For instance, reducing absenteeism by 20 percent, concerns an issue that does not require technical knowledge. Everybody knows what is involved. That does not mean that everybody can decide that 20 percent is the right amount of reduction to set as a goal, but everybody knows how absenteeism reduction will affect them and the other people involved.

Some seemingly trivial decisions, such as whether, or how, to allocate parking spaces, or change the coffee break time, also lie in this quadrant. In such high acceptance/low technical requirement decisions, staff members or their representatives should have the primary voice, whenever possible. It is obvious that any decision or plan, where people believe that they can make a useful contribution, and/or which affects them seriously will turn out better if high levels of participation can be used. If there are differences of opinion among group members, the manager must lead the group to a consensus that will bring the minimum resentment from dissenting individuals so that all will exert the greatest effort toward successful implementation. For this task, the skills for effective management of potentially damaging conflicts/disputes are, of course, needed (see Question 6.3).

Decisions and plans with low acceptance requirement/high technical requirement, clearly need the involvement of people (from inside the organization and/or from outside) who have the necessary technical expertise. Often these people can recommend the most appropriate action and the manager can approve it (after confirming that the acceptance requirement is really very low) possibly with no more that just informing staff members in sufficient detail. Whether the matter is on the low end of low acceptance requirement or near the high end, can make a big difference. If in doubt, it is better to err on the side of assuming that there is greater interest by staff members.

Finally, decisions and plans in the high acceptance requirement/high technical requirement area require the greatest skill on the part of the manager. Here there is the need for ensuring that the necessary technical competence is available, but also a need for convincing those with dissenting views to accept or preferably be convinced of the wisdom of the decision(s). For example: to quickly reduce the time needed to improve the reliability of a technical product may call for considerable technical knowledge to develop a realistic plan. Successful implementation, though, might require a high level of acceptance if the engineering department and the manufacturing departments have different views on how to best achieve the desired result.

The people who have the technical knowledge to determine what is feasible and/or likely to be most successful must recommend what should be done in these situations. Success of such decisions, and achievement of related goals, however, may require implementation by several or even many people. If the decisions and goals have high acceptance among these people, then the probability that challenging goals will be achieved is much higher than if such acceptance is lukewarm or lacking. After obtaining the advice of the experts, the manager therefore has to confirm that other staff members agree that the suggested alternatives are indeed the best course of action. If in doubt about such acceptance, the manager has to do everything possible to convince the group, possibly make adjustments, in effect 'selling' the direction recommended by the experts.

Question 2.1b—What Level of Work-Maturity is Required of a Participant in a Segment of a Decision or in an Entire Plan?

Work maturity is not a matter of age, but rather the extent to which the person, or group, can be counted on to accept responsibility:

- for their input, and
- for their respective roles in implementation.

Work maturity, of course, presupposes personal maturity. A person who is not mature in personal life is not likely to have mature norms and attitudes in work life.

Selection of participants requires that the manager assess this characteristic of potential participants, together with the technical or other contribution they can make. If more than one possibly qualified candidate is available, when important, it is usually advisable to select the one with greater work maturity.

As will become obvious in Chapters 6, 7, and 9, consideration should be given to assist less work-mature staff members to acquire the attributes of greater work maturity.

In addition to affecting the selection of participants, work maturity also affects the level of participation, and the selection of the segment of the decision or plan for the individual—the HOW and WHAT (see Question 2.2, below).

Question 2.2—*How,* and on *What* Part of the Decision or Plan Should the Participants be Involved?

The *what* refers to the fact, that in major decisions or plans, that involve complex issues, it would be appropriate to ask different individuals to participate in different issues. For instance, goals need to be set for teams and for individuals. For team goals, all members of the team could be called on to participate, possibly in different ways, while for the goals for individuals only the respective person would participate with the manager.

The answers to the *how* and *what* question determines what authority the manager or project leader should grant to each individual or group, and whether it should apply overall or to only one or more aspects.

In addition to the technical and acceptance requirement considerations, and the work maturity issues, to make appropriate selections, managers have to be aware of all the options available to them. That requires also looking at issues related to the specific situation. For these issues it can be useful to think of the Autocratic-Democratic Continuum (Tannenbaum & Schmidt, 1958/1973), and the Vroom and Yetton Leadership-Participation Theory (Vroom & Yetton, 1973).

Briefly, the Tannenbaum and Schmidt Autocratic-Democratic Continuum Model holds that the person leading the approach to a challenge can choose from many possible combinations between the two extremes of a) autocratic control in deciding alone what to do, and b) wide freedom by staff members or other participants to determining what should be done. For example, a manager can choose any one of the following, or even other participation levels between them:

- No contribution by staff members and/or other participants
- Responses only, to specific questions, from staff members and/or other participants
- Suggestions, comments and cautions only, from staff members and/or other participants
- A small voice in the actual decision/plan for staff members and/or other participants

- An equal voice with the manager for staff members and/or other participants
- A larger voice than that of the manager, for staff members and/or other participants, within limits specified by the manager
- Full authority to make the actual decision or develop the plan, for staff members and/or other participants, within limits specified by the manager

It probably is obvious that the more mature a staff member is, the greater the influence that person can be offered.

According to the Tannenbaum and Schmidt model, the most effective leaders are those who have the best batting average in choosing the most appropriate mix between 'Boss-centered' leadership, and 'Subordinate-centered' leadership (the terms actually used originally by the authors in 1958).

The Vroom and Yetton Leadership-Participation Theory is a refinement of the Autocratic-Democratic Continuum Model. It selects five specific points from the many possible ones along the continuum. A leader (the person with the primary responsibility for the decision or plan) should choose that point which is indicated on a decision tree, based on the answers to several questions which concern:

- The extent to which there is a technical quality requirement for the decision or plan
- The extent to which the leader has the needed information
- The extent to which structure (policies or procedures) determine alternatives and choice
- How acceptable a specific possible solution would be to the staff
- The extent to which the goals of the organization (or the outcome conditions) are shared by staff members, and
- The likelihood of conflict/disputes

Question 2.3—*When* Should the Person or Group be Invited to Participate?

Appropriate participation (please note that the emphasis is always on "appropriate") also involves timing—when each person or group should participate. With respect to a decision, beyond mere notification after it has been made, the 'when' range stretches from only requesting opinions after a tentative decision has been made, through some participation in almost every step of the process, to giving the staff members full authority right from the beginning: 'whatever you do will be OK with me'. The specific time when to meet for any discussion is, of course, also part of this issue. One guiding principle should be to vest the primary authority for the 'when' at the lowest level in the organization where adequate information and competence (and work maturity) is available.

In addition to determining who should participate, how, on what, and when, there are other questions (2.4 and 2.5) that might affect aspects of participation.

Question 2.4—Where Should the Contact Be?

Appropriate participation in one decision or plan, as has been pointed out before, can involve one or more people (staff members or others). Depending on the circumstances, if the contacts are to be face-to-face involving just the manager and one single staff member or several, they would be where such contacts would be most convenient for all involved. They can also be non-physical, on the telephone (possibly in conference calls) and in real-time electronic contacts. E-mail and messages, memos, or letters, can also serve as vehicles for appropriate participation, as well as any combination of the media mentioned. The point is that appropriate participation is not dependent on fixed locations, nor is it limited to personal contact. As is mentioned elsewhere (at the beginning of this chapter and in Chapter 4), appropriate participation does not require a venue for a meeting.

Question 2.5—What Are Other Elements of the Situation?

Strictly speaking, this could be considered an entire group of questions. For the sake of simplicity, the question can, however, serve as a reminder of the less important and not as frequently applicable issues that also apply to appropriate participation. These other aspects of the situation that can also influence participation include items suggested by the Vroom and Yetton model, and others. They are:

- The time and cost of participation (to the organization and to the participants)
- How strongly potential participants expect, or want to be, involved
- The likelihood of conflicts/disputes
- The information that is available or can be made available
- The influence of procedures and policies
- The impact on the participants, and
- The urgency and importance of the desired outcomes.

CHAPTER 6

QUESTION 3: COMPETENCE

What could or should to be done, if anything, to achieve the highest possible competence for every action?

(Question 3—A primary question)

SUBSIDIARY QUESTIONS PERTAINING TO COMPETENCE

There are three components to high-level competence: a) ensuring that competent people are selected for vacant positions (from internal and external candidates), b) that there is effective competence development and c) that best use is made of competence strengths. The first one of these refers, in part, to responsibilities which many managers face only rarely and that can frequently be eliminated during the initial identification of issues that are relevant to the respective situation.

Question 3.1—Who Should Be Considered for Vacant Positions?

To fill vacant positions, the search for candidates could consider both internal and external candidates. Some organizations prefer to look first among current members and others look to fill vacant positions with outsiders. There are valid points that can be made for either of these preferences.

Planning, Common Sense, and Superior Performance, pages 65–72

Promotions or transfers of current staff members for development purposes brings benefits in morale and commitment to the organization, but, of course, is somewhat restricted to existing competencies and could be limiting in viewpoint of the candidate to the organizational culture.

Outside candidates promise to bring fresh viewpoints and possibly useful intelligence about competitive organizations.

For selecting the best candidates, it is useful to pay as much attention to ability and motivation to learn, and attitudes toward cooperation, as to current level of skill, knowledge and work maturity (as defined in Chapter 5). For reassignment of existing staff members, most of the information for making selection decisions is available internally. Still interview records for such candidates may be necessary to at least partially protect against the possibility that someone might charge favoritism or discrimination.

Most organizations use the job descriptions, which contain the job requirements, as foundation for obtaining the relevant information for evaluation of external candidates. While these are useful for some aspects of the inquiry into the candidate's background, they are not adequate for evaluating and developing knowledge and skills, because they do not help to identify specific competence levels and learning needs. For that purpose, knowledge/skill profiles (see a. in Skills for Management of Learning in this chapter) can be most helpful. Some effort is required to prepare such a profile, if one does not exist, but it can be most rewarding, not only in selection but also in identifying learning needs and planning the learning that a person who is new in the respective position may need.

In the selection process, from recruiting through interviewing and final selection, attention also has to be paid to applicable federal and state laws and regulations on discrimination, wages and hours, privacy, etc.

Issues that should guide selection include:

- Ensuring that interviews (of external and internal prospects) are conducted competently, based not only on job experience, but also on level of desirable knowledge and skills, motivation for self-development, and favorable attitudes toward cooperation with people and procedures
- That the comparison between candidates is done as much as possible on an assessment of their respective potential
- Adherence to relevant laws and regulations

Question 3.2—What Staff and Manager Competence Deficiencies Need to be Addressed With Management of Learning, Coaching, and On-The-Job Training (OJT)

This question has application in almost every situation since thorough consideration of every problem, challenge, or opportunity, is likely to expose some opportunities for competence enhancement which deserve attention if the organization is to have the benefit of the highest possible competence level. It is also important to keep in mind that thinking about an organization's competence need not be limited to what is relevant to a specific situation. Beyond staff members involved, it could include consideration of other internal stakeholders as well as of external ones (such as internal and external clients/customers as in the case of external sales offices that might call on distributor staff members, and purchasing departments who might look to suppliers, where applicable).

Opportunities always exist to identify some competence deficiencies that could or should be reduced or eliminated. Development of skills and the underlying knowledge, can provide benefits beyond the immediate need, such as back-up capabilities and depth of staff competencies. That means that managers/leaders must be alert to opportunities and competent as managers of learning if they want to ensure that their organizations will always have the necessary competencies. This is especially important if their organizations or units are to be learning organizations (Senge, 1990), considered to be the new imperative of success.

Application of theories of learning, with emphasis on adult learners and specifics of learning assessment as well as use of appropriate delivery techniques, is basic to competence development. These require knowledge and skills for management of learning. They can also benefit from presentation skills, learning facilitation in meetings and with individuals, coaching, and on-the-job training. Only management of learning (see below) will be discussed here. The other topics are covered extensively in the education and training literature, and are beyond the scope of this book.

Question 3.3—How can Most Effective use of Competence Strengths be Achieved?

For highest overall competence, having the most capable individual in every position and on every project is of primary importance. Beyond selecting for vacant positions, there is the more frequent opportunity in effective selection for teams and projects that should take competence strengths into consideration. Such assignments deserve serious thought whenever a project, problem, challenge, or opportunity, involves the need to find someone to take the lead or to augment a team. For example, using staff members for coaching and on-the-job training of others, and for assignments to projects where their technical knowledge and skill will bring most effective and efficient progress, makes use of competence strengths. At the same time, it can contribute significantly to best possible performance of an organization. Essentially the same considerations apply there as for filling of vacant position and similar care should be devoted.

Both considerations (Questions 3.1 and 3.3), though they are of critical importance, do not apply to a large proportion of decisions/plans because they often will have been considered in prior, related or unrelated matters.

Beyond that, not much can be said in a general way about questions pertaining to the use of competence strengths, except, of course, to think of them when relevant. Much depends on the specific situation, respective strengths, and the needs of the organization. However, the habit of thinking of this issue may result in people with specific talents being placed strategically into positions, and tactically on teams and projects, where they will do the most good. This holds true whether the respective strengths are of a technical nature, or can enhance coaching/mentoring, client contact, better organization of work, a cheerful environment, etc.

At the same time, effective use of competence strengths adds to mutual trust between managers and staff members, because: staff members are assured that their manager is aware of their capabilities. They gain greater satisfaction because they are likely to enjoy their work more, they are more enthusiastic about self-development, and they make more effective, rewarding use of their skills and knowledge. Unfortunately too many organizations are like the armed services during wars, where people were placed without regard to their skills and other strength, strictly on the basis of where the most current or urgent need was believed to be.

Overlooking the competence strengths of staff members can be avoided if managers keep this consideration in mind when selecting for positions, teams, projects and even tasks.

SKILLS FOR MANAGEMENT OF LEARNING

Management of learning is different from teaching, primarily in perspective. First of all it applies to self-learning as much as to assisting others to learn. Teaching, in the most frequent use of the word, is the passage of information and conveying of skills, from one who knows, and can do, to those who need to know, and do, with lectures and other one-way techniques. Management of learning attempts to achieve the same results, more effectively, by stimulating motivation to learn. The manager of learning helps to identify specific learning needs and provides assistance to learners, as they strive to acquire competence. The difference is in the emphasis—in teaching it is on the learning content. In management of learning it is on the learner and on the process of acquiring competence.

The word 'teacher', though seemingly directly related to teaching, has a different connotation. 'Teacher' is a title. Most teachers do their best to help students learn by being facilitators who use management of learning concepts. Unfortunately there are also those who rely mostly on lectures, possibly with demonstrations of skills, by choice, and not because they face large classes without assistance, or for similar compelling reasons. In management of learning, curiosity and motivation to learn is stimulated by presenting only that portion of the material which learners can readily absorb. If presented in an interesting format, learners will reach out for more and greater competence.

Basically the management of learning concept is simple. It involves four questions:

1. What does the learner (do I, or other learners) need to learn?
2. What goals or priorities should be considered to best satisfy these needs?
3. What learning materials and experiences will be most effective in reaching the goals, and when, where, and how, should they be delivered?
4. How can accomplished learning best be measured (evaluated) and retention ensured?

The steps implied by these questions have to be repeated in an ongoing cycle as often as necessary, until full competence is achieved to apply what has been learned.

Managers/leaders who also want to be effective managers of learning, follow these steps themselves for their own learning. They help their staff members identify what they need to learn to become more competent, and then help them learn. This means that they have to arrange for attendance at fully appropriate programs, suggest self-study and practice steps, and provide feedback on learning progress. They may also have to do, or arrange, some direct coaching (including on-the-job-training), and provide appropriate recognition.

a. What Does the Learner (do the Learners) Need to Learn?—Using Self-Assessment Possibly with Knowledge/Skill Profiles

A manager and an organization that firmly stands behind a policy of competence development can benefit from encouraging the use of knowledge/skill profiles. These contain lists of topics that define the knowledge and skills—the competencies—required by a position, or by a major segment/function of a position. Each line on the profile represents either:

- A limited amount of knowledge that can be learned from a short presentation or discussion, by studying from a book, manual, or articles, or
- A skill that can be enhanced with a limited amount of practice

On every line there is space for entering the date by when the respective item is expected to have been achieved.

Most lines are likely to represent both, some knowledge and a skill. To be most useful, they are developed jointly by the person charged with assisting the learner (the manager or a coach) and the learner because the manager knows more about what has to be learned and the learner is likely to know more about his or her competencies and deficiencies.. Together they can ensure that all competencies are included. Setting the timelines by when a respective competency should be fully mastered is, of course, also a joint activity, as is reviewing progress on each line.

A training manager or someone else can create a knowledge/skill profile when there are several or many people in similar but not identical positions, or have similar projects. Then the profiles may have to be adapted to individuals. Profiles can also be useful for self-assessment by the manager and by professionals in unique positions.

b. What Goals or Priorities Should be Considered to Best Satisfy These Needs?

Little needs to be said about learning goals (completion dates) and priorities. They are no different than other goals and all the relevant points outlined in Chapter 11 apply.

c. What Learning Materials and Learning Experiences (Delivery Techniques for Information/Knowledge and Skills) Will be Most Effective in Helping Learners Reach the Competence Goals, and When and How Should They be Delivered?

There is a wide range of possible learning experiences that can be used singly or in combination, as the situation requires. With modern technology, more such choices exist, than ever before. These learning experiences, or methods, include: (many are available with and without multimedia support)

- Traditional classes or seminars with lectures, case studies, simulations, role-plays, and other team activities
- Traditional self-study with appropriate materials

- Learning-topic discussion and demonstration of the application of new knowledge, and hypothetical or real application sessions at meetings,
- Reflection, or other evaluation of learning
- Distance instruction (learning) on the internet, on electronic networks, or with individual PC programs, with all the features of traditional classes
- Supervised individual work-projects or field assignments
- "Action Learning'" techniques where learning is drawn from analysis of work projects and reflection on learning that had taken place or could have occurred
- Developmental work assignments
- Supervised co-operative team projects
- Coaching
- Traditional on-the-job instruction

An extensive literature exists for all these methods. Of special interest to those who have responsibility for human resource development are some of the fundamental concepts that apply to all learning experiences (Knowles, 1990). Together with the learning difficulty of the subject, and the wide variety of individual learner obstacles to learning (Rausch, 1978/85), they limit what can be accomplished at any one time.

One learning method that is not widely used can have significant potential value when there is a widespread need among staff members, especially when seminars or courses are not readily available, and formal in-house sessions cannot be justified. It consists of brief sessions in staff meetings. Such sessions can present good opportunities for discussion of needed knowledge, and possibly for some practice of important skills. These additions to staff meetings are easy to arrange, and do not take much time. Staff members with extensive competence in the respective topic can present the topic, help to move the discussion along, or serve as facilitators if the group is broken into two or more learning teams.

Timing of the respective learning experience deserves brief mention here. In a process of enhancing competence, a number of topics and skills need to be addressed. The order in which this is done is important and depends on priorities that should be set consciously, rather than by default—here too, knowledge/skill profiles can be helpful.

Specific discussion of any of the learning experiences is beyond the scope of this book. Even discussions of coaching and on-the-job-instruction, which are critical to manager responsibilities at all organizational levels, are not covered. For all of these, there is an extensive literature where information can be found.

d. How can Learning Accomplishment Best be Measured and Retention Ensured?

Measuring what has been learned and ensuring that learners retain the acquired knowledge and skill is relatively easy when competence in what has been learned can readily be demonstrated. That is true for much technical knowledge and for simple skills. All that is needed is to review at the conclusion of the learning experience, and at some later time, how well the learner remembers, and/or performs a task. However, if new learning involves application in many different types of situations, and especially if complex skills require the exercise of judgment, both immediate evaluation at the conclusion of the learning experience, and assessment of retention, are far more difficult and complicated. Tests, role-plays, and even analyses of case studies are barely adequate to give insights into what has been learned. That is where it is essential to help the learner (with reminders) monitor and evaluate competence over time. Only with continuing attention to the competence level reached, will full mastery be achieved.

CHAPTER 7

QUESTION 4: SATISFACTION

What could or should be done so that stakeholders can gain the highest possible level of satisfaction from the contemplated actions?

(Question 4—A primary question)

INTRODUCTION

Paychecks are what people live on—Recognition and praise is what they live for.

(from a slogan by Beyond Work, Santa Clara, CA)

Expressions of appreciation for the contributions of staff members can add significantly to their job satisfaction. In a similar way, showing such appreciation for actions of other stakeholders, suppliers, cooperating teams or organizations, even customers can be beneficial. Manager attention to that can go a long way to create and maintain a rewarding and motivational climate, one in which there is mutual trust and in which staff members develop a strong sense of belonging. For that reason, this question is one that should always be taken into account when a decision has to be made or a plan prepared. The discussion in this chapter could have used the word 'Recognition' in the relevant titles instead of 'signs (or evidence) of appreciation'. However, even though 'Recognition' is a popular word and will be used here frequently for lack of a fully meaningful one, it is not really appropriate. It implies an audience and hints at an outstanding accomplishment. There is no single word that conveys the expression of

Planning, Common Sense, and Superior Performance, pages 73–84

appreciation for contributions, including the non-spectacular but consistent ones, which are so important to staff member satisfaction.

Question 4.1—Is There a Need for More Appropriate and Adequate Psychological Rewards?[1]

It should be noted here that this question addresses primarily signs of appreciation for staff members that do *not* involve expenditures of money. Such signs of appreciation are critical to developing an atmosphere of mutual trust, of team spirit, and of positive discipline. For some detailed examples, please see the Appendix—Showing Appreciation.

The discussion in this chapter concentrates on staff members (with and without management/leadership responsibilities) reporting directly or indirectly to the manager. Signs of appreciation for contributions from other organizational units also deserve to be considered, especially for staff members with extensive outside contacts.

Research reported on in the literature supports the importance of recognition (Maslow, 1954; Herzberg, 1959, 1968; Alderfer, 1969; McClelland, 1961; Mayo, 1933, 1946; Deeprose 1994; Nelson, 1994, 1997, etc.; see also Reinforcement Theory (Steers & Porter, 1979; Skinner, 1968 in Chapter 14 under Motivation Theories). It is stated time and again that attention, and especially appropriate, honest, and regular feedback (positive when possible, and honest, factual when it pertains to errors), and recognition, are likely to stimulate positive discipline, adherence to desirable norms, and an accomplishment-oriented motivational climate.

Competent actions in showing appreciation for staff member contributions (recognition) bring a practical outcome—satisfying moments for the staff member. These moments, at least partially, balance the many negatives in the workplace—the dissatisfying moments that come from monotonous or disliked tasks, problems, errors, new restrictions, tight budgets, and conflicts/disputes.

Rewarding the members of your team for both their visible, and their less obvious accomplishments, is one important road to greater mutual trust and confidence. Show your people that you appreciate what they are doing, that you recognize the effort and thought they are devoting to making your team successful, and they will have greater confidence in you. Your work-life will be enriched by the pleasure you will gain from showing

---

1. For a detailed discussion of the issues in this question, see *Showing Appreciation*, in Section C of the Appendix)

appreciation and giving out awards, from better mutual understanding, and from helping them grow.

As manager you can reward the members of your team with more than just competitive incomes and benefits that your organization offers. You can help them enjoy a richer, more rewarding work-life by providing more frequent satisfying moments to counteract the impact of the negative minor and major events they face every day on the job.

To gain these benefits, you have to:

- Identify achievements,
- Use the many ways available to you for showing your appreciation fairly (and equitably, so it will not give the impression of favoritism) (in this book's Appendix, or Rausch and Washbush, 1998, or Carter and Rausch, 1999), and
- Overcome your concerns about showing appreciation (see Part C in this book's Appendix)

A word of caution: providing evidence of appreciation for staff member contributions should not be attempted as a device to manipulate them to work harder. The focus could be on helping them work smarter. Many staff members are skeptical of 'recognition' programs. Though they are inevitably pleased when appreciation is shown for one of their contributions, they can easily become cynical if they suspect that the purpose of showing appreciation is to manipulate them to greater effort.

Sincere evidence of appreciation, directed at specific accomplishments, but not shallow praise, will nevertheless undoubtedly lead to a more efficient team. Additional achievement may come in improved teamwork, better quality, greater attention to detail, better methods (smarter ways of doing the work) and widespread willingness by staff members to overlook, or downplay, the many annoyances that are unavoidable.

If you are perceived as insincere or as using superficial signs of appreciation to manipulate people, then relatively little is gained from showing appreciation. That is why competence in identifying staff member contributions and in applying the many possible ways to recognize staff members, is so important (see what staff members want in the discussion of Question 4.3).

Question 4.2—Is There a Need for Concern about Stress (Work-Related and Personal), and Intervention to Ensure That Work-Related Stress Does Not Exceed an Appropriate Acceptable Level?

There are two reason why 'stress' is discussed in this chapter:

1. Work-related stress is a major contributor to dissatisfying moments—in fact it can be a continuous source of such feelings. Moreover, excessive stress is damaging to performance.
2. Showing concern about a staff member's level of work-related stress, and helping to reduce it, demonstrates interest in the staff members feelings and thus provides a satisfying moment even before something is done to reduce excessive levels of such stress. (Stress resulting from personal problems is briefly discussed under "Counseling"—Question 7.3)

The ever-growing information load and the frequently tight deadlines place increasing demands on people in most occupations. In addition to stresses directly related to the work, are the uncertainties in today's environment that often raise questions about job security. Health, family, and financial matters, too, may contribute by adding other stresses that reduce tolerance to work-related ones.

With the many potentially dissatisfying moments at work, the manager's responsibility as leader is to strike an optimum balance between the needs of the work, and the damaging effect of the stress level. Many managerial decisions should therefore consider issues related to the impact on the stress level which each alternative presents. If managers/leaders wish to preserve or enhance staff member satisfaction with work in the organizational unit, they have to accept responsibility for monitoring stress levels and taking steps to reduce them when they become too intense.

Two primary work-related stress sources deserve attention:

- Work load
- Organizational plans and rumors that may affect job security, compensation, and benefits.

Work load, of course, needs to be considered. Interestingly, though, employees will accept considerably greater workloads when they are satisfied with their work and their environment and if these meet their psychological needs.

When there are organizational plans that may affect job security, compensation, and benefits, and when you become aware of rumors that may raise concerns, you can intervene directly and quickly. Such intervention might be in the form of meetings where the issues are explored and as much as possible is done to allay any concerns. Serious situations might require one-on-one counseling sessions (see the segment on counseling in Chapter 10.

You might want to ask, from time to time, what you could do, beyond what you are doing, to further reduce any undesirable work-related stress (within the limits imposed by ensuring that the department's progress is fully supported by each staff member.) Here it is useful to keep in mind that change, any change, may bring with it some significant stress for at least some staff members.

Like change and conflict, not all work-related stress is detrimental. Healthy competition is stressful. Still, up to the limit that an individual can tolerate, it can be quite beneficial. The key here is the limit. Really effective leaders have sensors in place to ensure that they become aware when stress levels are at, or beyond, an individual's limit and thus detract from the satisfaction that the staff member gains from the work. Like psychological sign of appreciation, becoming aware of an individual's stress, and taking steps to counteract any negative effects, helps to build bonds between manager and staff member. It leads to better communications and higher levels of trust.

How can you develop better sensors? Ask yourself whether your communications are sufficiently open so people will confide in you. Also enlist, formally or informally, the help of all staff members to alert you to those who are becoming overly stressed. In addition to workload and rumors there are many other sources of stress that you might keep in mind. They include feeling undervalued, deadlines, non-regular work that has to be done, having to take on other people's work (while they are out), lack of job satisfaction, lack of control over the working day, having to work long hours, frustration with aspects of the working environment, tight targets (even when reasonable), seeing others not pulling their weight, managers changing their minds about what they want to be done, lack of support from managers, feeling put-upon by managers, interruptions by colleagues or by managers, bullying behavior by managers, lack of support from colleagues, and bullying behavior by colleagues, and personal cell phones set to an obnoxiously loud ring.

The interesting thing about this list is that it points to many things that managers can do pro-actively, to avoid stress and, at the same time, add satisfying moments when they communicate their awareness of such factors, when relevant, and of the steps they are taking to neutralize them.

Question 4.3—What Other Issues Deserve Consideration?

Achieving a truly satisfying climate requires much more than adequate psychological rewards, and adequate compensation and benefits. In Maslow's Hierarchy of Needs (see Chapter 14), the most widely known motivation theory, complete job satisfaction requires that the higher needs of individuals are fulfilled—especially self-realization, but also esteem, status, and belonging and social needs. This means that a truly rewarding job is likely to demand that the manager satisfies all aspects of the Eight-Questions Model.

Informal surveys of staff members and managers, intended to determine their expectations found widespread agreement about what would make them feel good about going to work every morning, to a job where the day flies by quickly, and where they would prefer to finish what they are doing rather than leave on time. This agreement was seen when hundreds of participants in seminars were asked the following question:

> If you think back to positions you have held, or if you look at your current position, what did, or could your manager or supervisor do, without spending any money, that would have helped you to be more satisfied with your job?

The lists of answers to this question included, almost always, at least the following items:

1. More information about what is going on
2. More freedom to do the job as I want to do it
3. More say on decisions at an earlier time
4. More guidance when I want or need it
5. More recognition for what I do
6. Honest feedback on performance
7. No promises that won't or can't be kept
8. More knowledge by the manager (or supervisor) about what I am doing
9. More interesting assignments
10. Less over-the-shoulder looking
11. More support when I need it
12. More confidence in my abilities

This list, then, provides a conceptual foundation for actions that managers at all levels can take so staff members will be aware that they appreciate their contributions, and for helping to ensure a truly satisfying work environment with mutual trust. The list highlights the need to pay attention to all eight questions if an organization wishes to establish and maintain a climate in which all staff members can gain the highest level of satisfaction from, and motivation for, their work. For instance, all show the need for attention to Question 4 on staff satisfaction and thorough attention to communications. Effective joint planning or goal setting and appropriate participation contribute to 2,3,8,9,10,11 and 12 above; coordination and cooperation, and progress/performance reviews involve 1,4,6,7,8 and 11; and so on.

Question 4.4—Are Semi-Tangible and Tangible Rewards Appropriate and Adequate?

Three groups of ways to show appreciation for staff member contributions and accomplishments are:

- Non-tangible (intangible) signs of appreciation (psychological and stress). They were the subject of the first two subsidiary questions above.
- Semi-tangible signs of appreciation, and
- Tangible signs of appreciation

The latter two are discussed later in this chapter.

Question 4.5—Is There a Need for More Appropriate Frequency of Evidence of Appreciation (Non-Tangible/ Intangible, Semi-Tangible and Tangible)?

With respect to the frequency with which signs of appreciation and rewards should be considered it is important that neither too few nor too many instances of the various types of evidence of appreciation are shown. This is important for non-tangible awards as well as for tangible ones. Too few are obviously not desirable. Too many of either, or both, can lessen their impact and value.

There are no hard and fast rules to follow in showing non-tangible appreciation for achievements. One instance, once a week on average, or even more is usually OK if varied and truly sincere, while once every other month is undoubtedly too little.

One overriding principle that should be observed in showing appreciation is *fairness*. Nothing is more important in showing appreciation and in performance evaluation (see Chapter 8).

Question 4.6—Will Stakeholders, Other Than Staff Members, be Satisfied?

A discussion of management responsibilities, and of the questions to which they lead, would not be complete if it did not include thoughts about the impact of decisions/plans on stakeholders other than staff members. There are basically three such groups:

1. Internal clients/customers, and support groups/departments
2. External clients/customers
3. Other stakeholders

1. Internal Clients/Customers, Suppliers, and Support Groups/Departments

It should be obvious that satisfying the needs and views of departments which use information, other services, or materials, that your department provides (internal clients/customers) deserve to be taken into account with all relevant decisions/plans. The same is true with respect to departments who provide them to your organizational unit.

Less obvious may be the desirability to consider the needs of other organizational units who may be affected by one of your team's decisions. If expertise from such units is needed for a plan, they will, of course, be consulted. Appropriate participation in decisions, or information about them, is one important way to ensure their satisfaction—at least it will bring knowledge of any dissatisfaction, and hints for positive steps that could be taken. Often it might therefore be desirable to invite someone from these other groups to become involved, or to inform them promptly, if a decision or plan is likely to affect them.

Still less obvious are the benefits of providing some form of recognition at appropriate moments, or just from time to time, to staff members of other teams or departments whose contributions should be acknowledged. Such recognition helps to lay the foundation for greater cooperation and coordination and, in general, for better communications. Not the least, it is likely to bring reciprocal steps from these other units (departments or teams), as mentioned previously.

2. External Clients/Customers

Matters affecting clients and customers are so central to an organization's performance that it is hardly necessary to mention that their views should be considered with every decision and plan affecting them directly.

As the many newsletters from organizations demonstrate, the benefits of informing external clients and customers of new developments often can be significant, for many promotional and goodwill reasons. In fact, other than good quality of products or services, the single most important factor for bringing satisfaction to these stakeholders, is accurate and timely information on matters of possible concern to them.

3. Other Stakeholders

The last group of stakeholders to consider is not a single group—it includes many groups: suppliers, neighbors, the community, regulators, other relevant government agencies, and even society as a whole. This is not the place to discuss specifically when and how it would be appropriate to consider the impact of decisions/plans on these stakeholders. It should be clear, however, that they too deserve a place if the initial assessment of relevant issues shows some possible effect on them.

The conclusion is that, in the early assessment of relevant responsibilities, the issues pertaining to internal and external stakeholders deserve brief thought. That might possibly bring some ideas for plan components or goals and actions, as well as for items that should be added to the requirements for a desirable outcome.

PROVIDING SEMI-TANGIBLE SIGNS OF APPRECIATION

Semi-tangible signs are of three main types:

1. Memos and letters
2. Certificates and plaques
3. Trophies

1. Memos and Letters

These can originate from the same sources as non-tangible signs of appreciation. You have full control over the memos and letters that come from you. You also have considerable control over those that come from the higher-level managers, and you can make arrangements with other departments to ensure their cooperation. Memos and letters from outsiders can also be stimulated.

2. Certificates and Plaques

These are most appropriate for departmental accomplishments on formal programs such as *Most Days Without Accident, Most Days Without Absences, Most Units Without Defects*, or other team awards on various goals or achievements, including those on safety, attendance and quality.

For individual accomplishments they are appropriate for programs such as *Staff Member of the Week/Month/Year* and for more specific accomplishments, in some environments, especially those where customers or members of the public can see them.

Certificates and plaques are best for staff members who have their own offices or private spaces where they could display them. They can sometimes be mounted in a central, highly visible area, together with all other recent ones. Some organizations have large plaques for certain awards that many staff members can achieve and there are small cards with their names.

A caution: In all likelihood, certificates will only be appreciated in an environment where staff members are proud of them and actually want to display them.

3. Trophies

Trophies are similar to plaques. They lend themselves best to departmental accomplishments. For presentations to individuals, the environment must be one in which staff members are proud of such evidence of appreciation and will actually display them.

PROVIDING TANGIBLE SIGNS OF APPRECIATION

There are several types of tangible signs of appreciation in each of these major groups:

- Salary increases
- Bonuses
- Compensatory time
- Monetary awards
- Merchandise and travel awards

The first three may come automatically in accordance with formal procedures such as compensation or incentive programs, or they may be at the discretion of the manager.

Decisions on the compensation structure that controls the salary increases and bonuses must balance many factors. (Rausch, 1978/1985). These considerations are primarily functional issues for high level managers and for those in human resources departments who have authority or responsibility for recommendations on these matters.

Your involvement in tangible rewards is likely to be primarily in three areas:

- In your role in which you may be responsible for allocating any salary and departmental bonus budgets to your staff members. Here is where you face the difficult task of tying performance evaluation to personnel actions. Unfortunately there are few guidelines that you can follow, beyond those that are discussed in Chapter 8. However, these tangible rewards are usually communicated only to the recipients, but they have significant impact on perceptions of organizational justice.
- Compensatory time is usually based on established practice and certainly has to be granted in a fair and equitable manner without favoritism or bias
- The situation is different with monetary and monetary-equivalent achievement awards (merchandise and travel, or points which can be collected and then exchanged for these). If they are not part of a for-

mal incentive program, they are usually presented at staff meetings. How you conduct such meetings can make a difference to their impact.

- There may be some tangible rewards you can use, that would not run counter any organizational policy, which would also not set an undesirable precedent. They could include inviting one or several employees for lunch at a good restaurant, or merchandise gifts. Avoiding perception of favoritism is, of course, important.

TEN STEPS FOR SHOWING APPRECIATION OF ACCOMPLISHMENTS WITH INTANGIBLE SIGNS OF APPRECIATION, AND SEMI-TANGIBLE AWARDS

1. Provide informal acknowledgements as soon as you become aware of a deserving action or accomplishment.
2. Set aside a few moments each week to write down accomplishments by staff members that deserve notice, in addition to any oral acknowledgements that have already been provided.
3. Continue your list with positive actions and accomplishments, which would go unnoticed without the preparation (and availability) of this list. Consider all activities that enhance departmental or organizational performance:
   - general activities
   - activities specific to the staff member's work
   - activities in interpersonal relations
   - behavior based on personal characteristics

   Do not make the list overly long and review earlier items to avoid duplication.
4. Decide on the level of appreciation you might consider for each specific accomplishment.
5. Act on the verbal and written signs of appreciation that you want to use.
6. Where applicable, enlist the aid of higher level managers and managers in other departments, for oral and written signs of appreciation.
7. Where applicable, review what additional steps can be taken to gain cooperation from customers or members of the public, and implement these steps.
8. Prior to each award presentation, make final decisions on specific signs of appreciation to award.

9. Conduct an informal presentation ceremony fairly regularly. Make the annual and semi-annual presentations more formal and include the tangible awards.
10. At every ceremony, think of those who do not receive an award, and focus your remarks on them in such a way that they, too, will gain satisfaction from the session.

CHAPTER 8

QUESTION 5: PROGRESS AND PERFORMANCE REVIEWS AND PERFORMANCE EVALUATIONS

What could or should be done, if anything so that greatest benefits can be derived from progress and performance reviews, and performance evaluations?

(Question 5—A Secondary Question)

This question, possibly even more so than Question 6 is relevant only if it has not been adequately considered in conjunction with previous decisions/plans. Once the procedures and policies have been set up including monitoring of adherence, they need to be thought of only occasionally and when something happens that questions their adequacy. That is necessary because effective and appropriate use of these leadership/management activities is important to most effective accomplishment of routine work and of work toward projects, plans and goals.

Though they sound like very similar activities, performance evaluations, and even performance reviews are quite different from progress reviews. They are, however, related activities. While it is beneficial for managers to conduct progress and performance reviews at frequent occasions, the evaluations are formal activities that occur fairly rarely (one to four times per year).

Planning, Common Sense, and Superior Performance, pages 85–89

In light of the potential impact on performance, questions pertaining to reviews, and sometimes even of evaluation, when relevant, may deserve inclusion in the desired outcome of a decision or plan.

Question 5.1—Are Progress Reviews Used Effectively?

For sound communications and to help cement trust between manager and staff member, fairly frequent informal discussions, in the form of progress reviews, are highly desirable on all projects, goals and plans. Emphasis should be a) on obtaining information on status from the staff member, and b) on discussion of any need for manager support and/or the desirability for a change in direction if difficulties have arisen. Frequency of progress reviews depends on the situation, especially on complexity of the project/goal/plan, and maturity/competence of the manager or staff member responsible for the project.

Question 5.2—Are Performance Reviews Used Effectively?

Performance reviews are very similar to progress reviews, except that they concern performance on regular, ongoing duties, and discussions about opportunities for improvement. These reviews also present an opportunity to gain insight into a staff member's personal norms. Frequency of performance reviews may be set by organizational procedure or up to each manager. They are likely to be more regular than progress reviews, being scheduled for once a month or two, because they concern ongoing activities. They can also be beneficial on specific elements of performance when either something laudable occurs, or when there is a problem with the staff member's performance.

Frequent progress and performance reviews are the foundation of what is often called performance management. Though brief and informal, competent managers discuss:

- Any challenges with the regular, ongoing work
- Progress on projects, goals and plans that have not yet been achieved
- New performance improvement goals that may be needed or advisable, as a result of new challenges that have arisen, or of opportunities of which either the staff member or the manager became aware, and
- Any support that may be needed from the manager

The reviews may also identify topics on which most or all staff members may need some training or refreshers. As pointed out in Question 3.3, Chapter 6, if seminars or courses are not readily available, brief sessions in staff meetings can present good opportunities for discussion of the topic, and possibly for some practice.

Question 5.3—Are Performance Evaluations (Assessments) Used Effectively?

> Organizations can ill afford to let injustice be ignored,
> Though it may cause them some surprise, to find where fairness really lies.
> We know less clearly what is meant by justice, than be discontent
> And so, the search for justice leads to balancing desert with needs.
> —Adapted from Kenneth Boulding, *Principles of Economic Policy*, 4

Progress and performance reviews are informal. They do not affect the staff member's employment record, though they are a source of information for possible informal performance feedback.

Performance evaluations (sometimes referred to as assessments), in contrast to the reviews, are formal, usually infrequent occurrences, conducted once to four times per year. They are most likely to be thorough and meaningful if they are based on the exchange of information that has occurred during the progress and performance reviews. Even though their primary objective should be the development of, and agreement on, performance improvement plans they are likely to have an impact on compensation elements and on career opportunities. For these reasons, fairness is essential to prevent injustice. However, as the lead-in poem points out, fairness has many facets and is difficult to fully accomplish in practice, as briefly discussed under Obstacles to performance evaluation, below. (Armstrong, 2000; Didactic Systems, 1974; Bacal 1998).

REQUIREMENTS FOR EFFECTIVE PERFORMANCE EVALUATION (ADAPTED FROM RAUSCH, 1985, 1996; SEE ALSO ARMSTRONG, 2000)

As pointed out above, to be effective, performance evaluations must be *fair* (and thus contribute to organizational justice), first and foremost. To be most useful, they should focus on performance improvement and conclude with a jointly developed performance improvement plan.

Since fairness depends greatly on the perceptions of those who are being evaluated, the evaluations must avoid anything that might be perceived as favoritism. To be fair, and be perceived as fair, they should satisfy the requirements below, and the person being evaluated, should be aware that these criteria are being used.

Thorough

- Performance of all staff members is measured similarly
- Evaluations measure all responsibilities
- Evaluations measure performance for the entire period (regular reviews provide this information)

Accurate and Factual

- Evaluation standards cover all responsibilities
- Evaluation standards are accurate and factual
- There is little or no ambiguity
- Evaluations are comparable between evaluators
- Evaluations are reviewed by at least one manager who has detailed independent knowledge of the staff member's work, or by an equivalently independent source

Meaningful

- Evaluation standards and evaluations consider the importance of each function
- Evaluation standards and evaluations attempt to measure primarily matters under the control of the staff member
- Feedback and/or evaluations occur at regular intervals or at appropriate moments
- Managers continue to improve skills in applying the requirements for effective evaluation
- Evaluation results are used for important personnel decisions, especially those that pertain to compensation decisions and selection of candidates for vacant positions that might be of interest to staff members

Satisfy Needs

- Evaluation standards are communicated in advance
- Staff members are kept informed about their performance
- Communications are factual, open, and honest
- Evaluation standards are challenging but realistic
- Staff members are directly or indirectly involved in setting of standards and in the evaluations

- Evaluations consider the adequacy of the manager's support
- *Evaluation emphasizes competence development* (this may be the most important element for managers to keep in mind)

Appeals

- An appeals procedure exists

PERFORMANCE EVALUATIONS, ORGANIZATIONAL JUSTICE, AND TRUST

Performance evaluations are probably the most difficult of all management/leadership tasks. Still, sound and fair assessments stimulate motivation for specific learning and skill development. Possibly even more important, are their critical roles in helping to achieve coordination and cooperation and their vital role in helping to shape a satisfying work environment.

Only considerable mutual trust, built on honest and open communications will bridge the many potentials for serious conflict of perceptions, and of basic interests, in performance evaluations. Unfortunately, trust is not easy to achieve, especially for a manager who does not have exceptional talent for communicating (and thus can demonstrate the rare quality of charismatic leadership.) However, honest feedback on performance, including progress on projects, delivered in timely reviews, and performance evaluations that are perceived as *fair* and concentrate on competence development, can go a long way toward establishing mutual trust.

CHAPTER 9

QUESTION 6: COORDINATION, COOPERATION, AND CONFLICT

What could or should be done, if anything, so that the highest possible level of coordination and cooperation will be achieved, and conflict (disputes) be minimized?

(Question 6—A secondary question)

For smooth implementation of many decisions and plans, this sixth of the eight Questions can have significant impact. We often speak of coordination and cooperation in one breath, without making a distinction between these two activities. However, there are big differences and they invoke different specific matters to think about.

Question 6.1—How Can Best Coordination be Achieved?

Good coordination requires that all resources (people, financial, and equipment and materials) are available where and when needed, and that all actions are taken as expected. That depends primarily on sound procedures, thoroughly communicated and understood, so that all who are involved know what their respective roles and responsibilities are.

Coordination also requires willingness by everyone to follow the procedures—not only those that pertain to their own work, including matters

Planning, Common Sense, and Superior Performance, pages 91–95

that need to be completed at specific times. They also pertain to those that affect others, such as possibly timing of breaks or communications requirements. That is where one aspect of cooperation comes in—cooperation with the coordination procedures. That might be a reason why these two topics are so closely linked.

Effective coordination does not require that all procedures be in writing. Some should be, especially those that are not routine and therefore need a reference source. All, and especially the written ones, however, require monitoring, updating, and sharpening with time. For these reasons, coordination considerations deserve a quick assessment in most if not all decisions and plans, to see whether those that are relevant may need updating, and whether some aspect of coordination should be included in the determination of desirable outcome characteristics.

As was pointed out in Chapter 4, timely 360 degree communications in appropriate forms with all stakeholders, are of utmost importance in helping to ensure that everyone knows what is to be achieved and when, and what the respective roles of staff members are. Only with that information can there be full coordination and cooperation.

So that procedures are thoroughly communicated and updated when indicated, it is generally a good idea to consider the impact of any change in operations or staffing on any relevant written procedure, and to immediately review a procedure whenever even the slightest problem occurs which may affect it. This is where considering coordination in decisions and plans can be extremely helpful, by providing a reminder to review the relevant procedure so that similar, or even bigger problems can be prevented.

The views of staff members with respect to specific procedures always deserve consideration. In staff meetings, and during discussions involving one or several persons, feedback can be solicited on relevant procedures, thus providing a foundation for changes that might be desirable.

In summary, it is useful to quickly assess whether any coordination issues are relevant to a situation and, if there are some, to take them into account. In all probability, thinking of coordination will also bring a quick review of the communications necessary for coordination, and their implementation.

Question 6.2—How Can the Highest Level of Cooperation Be Achieved?

While coordination concerns primarily concrete issues, cooperation involves perceptions. It is the result of willingness, and therefore depends on attitudes toward the people with whom to cooperate, on the matters or procedures for which cooperation is desired, and especially with change—

when new procedures and staffing issues are being discussed and/or put in place.

Most important are early identification of cooperation problems, and prevention or effective resolution, of all potentially damaging conflicts/ disputes. (See below)

In addition, most of the other questions in the Eight-Questions Model influence cooperation:

- Thorough communication, as mentioned earlier in this Chapter, and discussed in Chapter 4, is critical to cooperation because it influences the feeling of community and belonging, among stakeholders. Furthermore, when communication issues are addressed effectively, they help to strengthen trust and confidence, major foundations for cooperation.
- Appropriate participation, (see Chapter 5), the involvement of staff members, leads to willingness or even desire to cooperate with the implementation of the respective decision or plan.
- Recruiting and selection of people with cooperative values and favorable past records, as Chapter 6 suggests, provides a sound foundation for cooperation. The same applies to selection of staff members for teams and projects.
- Chapter 8, Progress and performance reviews, and performance evaluations, presents other questions that also have considerable impact on cooperation. If thought of cooperation enters the decisions pertaining to every review and evaluation, the result cannot help but be beneficial in strengthening coordination and cooperation.
- The issues in Chapter 10, Norms, ethical policies/behavior positive discipline, and counseling, as will be seen, have considerable effect on cooperation. If the norms of cooperation are strengthened with every decision, and if they are considered in counseling, greater cooperation is likely to result. Norms of cooperation also provide one of the foundations of positive discipline.
- Goals and plans, if managed with consideration for the issues covered in Chapter 11 will enhance cooperation.

Question 6.3—How Can Potentially Damaging Conflicts/Disputes Best be Prevented or Managed?

Giving early thought to the possibility of potentially damaging conflicts, between individuals, teams, or departments that might arise during, and in the wake of a decision or plan, can often be beneficial. Though some conflict such as friendly competition is not damaging, unfortunately, most conflicts bring damaging effects. The best way to handle the latter types of conflicts/disputes is to prevent them in the first place. When a conflict cannot be predicted and therefore will arise, the next best approach is to recognize it early, when it might be easiest to manage/resolve (Whetten & Cameron, 1993). For these reasons, thought of possible conflict has been included in this question.

For an organization to best manage conflict. it is useful for all members to think of themselves as managers of conflict—individuals who have active internal mediators. This means that, while they keep their point of view and interests in mind they also assume some of the role of a mediator in assisting the conflict/dispute resolution process to proceed as smoothly as possible. These two roles may seem to be mutually exclusive, but that is not the case. A review of the process outlined below, shows that there is no need to drop one's point of view and interests, while watching the process, and helping it to move along.

The process of conflict management (and also of mediation) involves the following steps (Rausch & Washbush, 1998; Carter & Rausch, 1999):

1. Preventing or reducing undesirable emotions (by all participants in the conflict; there are indeed steps that one can take, in addition to staying calm, to help the opposing party to reduce expressions of negative emotions)
2. Identifying the issues of real importance (the interests) to the parties in the conflict, and separating them from the positions as stated by the parties[1]
3. Identifying possible solutions
4. Negotiating to find the best solution with consideration for the views of the parties, and of others who are significantly affected by the outcome of the conflict. This means working toward a win–win solution, couseling acceptance of compromise if necessary, possibly after postponement to allow time for everyone to gain a clearer view, or suggesting the use of a third party (mediator or arbitrator such as a higher level manager, or an outside arbitrator if all other approaches fail). In rare situations, considering conceding and accepting the other side's requests if it becomes clear that such a short-run loss is likely to lead to greater favorable long-term results such as good will.

---

1. Positions are what the parties say they want; interests are broader and more fundamental and rarely expressed. For instance, in union/management negotiations, what are the positions and what are the fundamental interests? Or, in bargaining for an antique—what are the positions and interests, respectively?

5. Implementing the best solution, including communicating it to those who are affected by it though they are not among the parties
6. Follow-up to monitor how well the outcome has helped to completely end the dispute.

The approach discussed above is, of course, not the only one that can be used. In their best-selling book "Getting to Yes", Roger Fisher and William Ury (1981), of the Program on Negotiations at Harvard Law School, suggest a different, somewhat more elaborate approach. That book and a follow-up volume by William Ury (1991), entitled "Getting Past No", present another very useful perspective.

While use of authority should be avoided as much as possible, in some instances, a party to a conflict or a conflict manager has to use position authority. In the case of parents, authority often works to the long-run benefit of both parties. The same can happen in a work environment.

When either party to a conflict is not in a position of authority over the other, authority can still be used in a conflict. One side may refuse to listen or agree to a course of action, rightfully or wrongfully withhold an object or service wanted by the other party, demand a postponement of the discussion when the postponement benefits one side, or just refuse to cooperate with further attempts to resolve the problem. Using authority that way may also be the best strategy in the rare instances when one side wants the responsibility for the outcome to rest solely with the other side. The party that uses authority can "win," for the moment at least, but the temporary advantage can also lead to negative effects, especially if it triggers retaliation from the adversary.

A manager should ensure that all the members of the organizational unit understand how to be managers of conflict and create a climate in which they want to apply this skill. Then most conflicts will have a happy ending. Conflict managers are wise to also consider issues that might bring new conflicts in the wake of resolved ones:

- The long-range impact of the solution (bitter experiences have shown, time and again, that short-term gain may lead to long-term loss, and vice versa.)
- The effect of the settlement on potential future conflict(s)
- The outcome's likely impact on individuals and groups who are not parties to the dispute

CHAPTER 10

QUESTION 7: NORMS, ORGANIZATIONAL JUSTICE, ETHICS, POSITIVE DISCIPLINE, AND COUNSELING

What could or should be done, if anything, to stimulate or maintain appropriate norms, organizational justice, ethical policies/behavior, positive discipline, and competent counseling?

(Question 7—A secondary question)

This group of questions is likely to be relevant only from time to time because most pertain to matters that change only very slowly. Still, the impact of existing norms and positive discipline might be worth considering with many decisions and plans. However, once plans or programs are in place to improve them, this question might not be among the relevant ones for some time.

Question 7.1—What is the Leader's Role in Ensuring Appropriate Norms, Organizational Justice, and Positive Discipline?

The word "norms," as far as the discussion in this book is concerned, refers to attitudes—the beliefs of people that pertain to:

Planning, Common Sense, and Superior Performance, pages 97–101

- The organization's and the leader/manager's views of organizational justice (Cropanzano, 1993; Greenberg, 1993)
- The organization's and the leader/manager's approach toward staff and performance
- Personal work/performance standards
- Personal behavior rules/code, ethics, life philosophy, including tolerance of viewpoints and of other people (gender, age, and ethnic or culture)
- Other matters that involve views on 'right or wrong' such as the 'golden rule'.
- Cooperation with (adherence to) laws, regulations, procedures, and with other people (managers, other employees, customers, suppliers, etc.—all stakeholders)

Personal norms, of course, include religious beliefs, opinions on what is just and fair, and other personal values. They reflect themselves in expressed or silently kept views, as well as in behaviors and *actions.* Possibly the easiest place to see norms at work is in the peer pressures on youngsters to conform with the group's norms. Norms can be seen in choice of clothing and personal appearance. These can be considered group norms.

At work there are basically three types of norms: a) those that are espoused and communicated by management; b) those that are held by staff members which correspond to the management norms, and c) norms held by staff members that do not match, or even oppose, the management norms.

It is the responsibility of all leaders/managers to be aware of these three types of norms as they exist in their organizations. That is not an easy task and the third type is likely to be known only to those managers who have established a fairly high level of mutual trust with the members of their staffs.

To identify norms, one can use, in addition to the golden rule, questions such as: Is it fair? Who gets hurt? Would it be embarrassing if it became public? Would you advise others, especially children to do it that way?

For changing undesirable norms, training programs and even counseling staff members may not be adequate. Assistance of other team members may be needed since peer pressure is probably the most effective approach. Being an effective role model, maintaining open two-way communications, and rewarding behavior that reflects appropriate norms, will also help. In addition, it is beneficial for managers to explain, from time to time, the reasons and benefits of the norms, which they believe would be most useful to the organization and to its members. It behooves managers to keep the conclusions from the Maier concept (see Question 2.1a), on matters requiring high acceptance in mind when trying to align personal norms by individuals or groups with organizational norms.

Higher level managers should consider, the first time the issue of norms is relevant, and again from time to time, whether the organization has, and communicates, ethical and just values They also should consider, from time to time, whether they and lower level managers have adequate competencies for identifying norms and for developing effective approaches to change norms that are not in the best interest of the organization and of the individuals who hold them. This is one area where outside professional assistance for training or possibly even coaching and counseling might be desirable.

Question 7.2—How Can the Highest Level of Positive Discipline Be Established and Maintained?

Positive discipline is the discipline of a team that wants to 'win'. In sports such discipline is almost a universal characteristic. It is also easy to see when a team 'wins'. Not necessarily so in organizations where the competitive element is not so direct and where 'winning' or 'losing' are complex matters, not easily determined most of the time. Yet, there, the willingness of individuals to set aside their personal interests, desires, and needs, for the benefit of the team's or organization's interests, may be just as important. Underlying this willingness are positive shared norms, and, of course, the absence of conflicts/disputes. That is why norms, and the anticipation/prevention/resolution of damaging conflict are so important to positive discipline (See Question 6.3 in Chapter 9). In fact, the level of positive discipline depends on the extent to which staff member personal norms are congruent with shared work-related norms and with those that management espouses.

Most people are uncomfortable when they hear the word discipline. To many it is almost a synonym for punishment. Some even hear 'punishment' when the word is used to describe tight authoritarian controls. To them it implies criticisms or penalties for individuals who do not meet standards or adhere to rules and accepted practices.

Positive discipline does not have such negative connotations. Managers who strive to achieve and maintain it do not resort to coercion (usually in the form of application of the organization's disciplinary procedure[1]) until *after* all other measures, including efforts at persuasion and formal counseling, have failed.

When there is positive discipline, the members of the organization know what is to be achieved. They voluntarily, even eagerly, subordinate personal interests to those of the team. In this environment, trust between leader and team is strengthened and discipline is:

- A common understanding of the rules of the game and of the standards of performance (the norms, including those for morality and diversity, for work ethic, for quality and security, for cooperation and for behavior limits)
- Awareness of the personal and team benefits of the rules and standards
- Willingness, on the part of individual team members, to make personal sacrifices, if necessary, to help the team achieve its goals and to adhere to the norms.

There are many things managers can do to bring about a climate of positive discipline. Effective application of the entire 8-Questions Model is important and especially accommodating staff member expectations with respect to the items mentioned in the list under Question 4.3. All this, when combined with the manager being an effective role model, will bring the highest level of mutual trust possible—and trust is another major building block of positive discipline.

Unfortunately there are some individuals in most organizations who consistently violate one or several of the norms that are fundamental to appropriate behavior. When an individual does that, counseling and possibly the use of the disciplinary procedure is indicated (Magoon & Richards, 1966).

Question 7.3—Where and When Might Counseling Be Needed?

There are four uses for counseling. The first two concern:

1. Work-related opportunities, challenges or problems
2. Self-development and learning challenges.

These two involve matters where the willingness of the staff members to do what is desirable or necessary, is likely to be a major reason for counseling. The possible need for counseling in these two situations should be

1. disciplinary procedures vary in content and formality, of course. Most, however, involve steps such as a) informal discussion (or more formal counseling) to explain what rules were violated, why the rules are reasonable and important, and why it is necessary that everyone respects them b) verbal warning(s), c) written warning(s), d) possibly suspension, and e) dismissal

considered in every decision and plan where the initial assessment has shown positive discipline to be relevant, because staff members frequently need guidance so they will be aware of, and adopt appropriate behavior or courses of action.

The other two concern:

3. Staff member career decisions. There the manager has a distinct, though more limited role to explain possible opportunities within the organization. If they are of interest to the team member, the manager can help the staff member become aware of competence requirements of aspired positions, and even guide her or him on how to gain such competencies, possibly by providing assistance—especially if that will lead to gaining increased depth of competence for the team.

   If a staff member seeks advice on a career change to work or positions that are not available in the organization, the manager's role is more sharply limited. It depends on the manager's knowledge of such work. However, in discussing the staff member's interests, the manager has to satisfy two major considerations: a) that there is a potential liability in giving advice that may lead to an unhappy outcome, and b) that taking a serious interest in being as helpful as possible has positive consequences on trust and morale, especially if the team member decides to remain with the organization.
4. Personal issues of concern to staff members, which do or may, affect performance. Here the manager's/leader's role is even more sharply limited since giving advice is potentially even more dangerous than career advice and can lead to liability of the manager and the organization if such advice backfires.

These second two uses of counseling apply only in situations where it appears that they might possibly be useful or desirable. When conducted competently, and cautiously they can help with maintaining a positive discipline climate because their effect is likely to further strengthen positive bonds between manager and staff member. Referring to the Human Resources department, to a higher-level manager, or engaging professional assistance, may be indicated.

All four uses, of course, require skills, as does the establishment and maintenance of positive discipline, and the alignment of norms. Discussion of these skills is beyond the scope of this book but there is an extensive literature and some coverage in the precursors to this book (Rausch 1978/1985; Rausch & Washbush, 1998).

CHAPTER 11

QUESTION 8: GOALS AND PLANS

Goals[1] and plans—what, if anything, could or should be done about possible use of goals to achieve the desired outcome?

(Question 8—A secondary question)

This eighth question of the model is called a secondary one because most of the issues (those that pertain solely to formal goals) apply only to some organizations.

For thorough discussions of what make goals programs successful, see *Balancing Needs of People and Organizations—The Linking Elements Concept*, (Rausch, 1978/1985) How to make a goals program successful, *Training and Development Journal*. (Rausch, 1980), and books by Barnard (1938), Odiorne (1968) and Locke (1984/90).

Our policy, to be effective,
Must chase a suitable objective,
So our economy should be
Both Growing, Stable, Just and Free.
The Dog would surely be a Dunce
Who tried to chase four things at once,
Yet that is just the way we plan
The task of Economic Man

—Adapted from Kenneth Boulding,
Principles of Economic Policy, 1

1. Though there are various definitions for the two words *goals* and *objectives* in the literature, the words are used interchangeably in this book

Planning, Common Sense, and Superior Performance, pages 103–128

As you ramble on through Life, brother,
Whatever be your Goal,
Keep your Eye upon the Donut
And not upon the Hole
—Cover of the Mayfair menu, (New York Coffee Shops)

INTRODUCTION

Much of this chapter applies primarily to organizations that are now working with formal goals, or contemplate the use of such goals. However, some of the issues discussed deserve consideration when plans are prepared for reaching the desirable outcome conditions. This applies specifically to Questions 8.3a through 8.3f (see below).

Desired outcomes of solutions to problems, for meeting a challenge, or exploiting an opportunity can be thought of as goals. For each outcome, plans are needed and they may involve one or more specific goals and several or many decisions. That raises the issues discussed in this chapter after the Introduction. They concern whether goals should be considered for the respective decision, the characteristics of effective goals, and their competent use. Attention to these issues differentiates organizations that are serious about using goals to help improve organizational performance, from those who merely have paper procedures pertaining to goals, but do not use goals competently.

An effective, coordinated system of long-term and short-term goals for the organization, organizational units and individuals, sets direction for them. It can also bring high achievement standards while, at the same time, ensuring that attention is paid to the competence needs of the organization and that a work environment is maintained that is as satisfying as possible. The longest-range goals are, in effect, what many call the 'vision' of the organization. The shortest-range goals are usually those that are set by, with, and for, individual staff members or small teams. It is important to realize that these goals in the really effective organization or organizational unit are rarely set by the manager alone, but rather reflect decisions arrived at as a result of appropriate participation, as was hinted at in Chapter 3 and as discussed in depth in Chapter 5.

It should be noted here again, that the what of goals (what goals to set) is likely to involve technical issues more than non-technical ones. However, the how to set goals (what steps to take when setting goals and what to consider to give the goals high quality and usefulness) is almost exclusively a matter of leadership-in-management—a non-technical issue.

Goals exist at all levels of an organization, whether all staff members, some, or none, know them, and whether or not they are part of the management and leadership system. In some organizations they are only ideas in the minds of some managers. In others they are paper tigers, used primarily to communicate lofty ideals and dreams. In still others, they are used in attempts to bring greater productivity, either coercively or voluntarily. Many organizations have some sort of formal goals program that is either successful, or limps along, partly ignored, and partly used to satisfy procedural requirements. Still, every staff member works, in one way or another, on matters that contribute to her/his goals, to the goals of the department and to the organization's goals.

It is important to realize that a goals program is not essential. Many organizations manage well without a formal or smoothly working one. Goals, which are aligned at all levels, can be of great help in ensuring coordinated efforts toward important matters. Still, working without a formal goals program is better than forcing a poorly understood and implemented one on an organization or organizational unit. There are, however, two places where goals are very important for effective management. These are: a) to thoroughly communicate when delegating, so that misunderstandings will be avoided; and b) to ensure that there is progress on continuing improvement in all functions of the organization or organizational unit. It is important to understand, furthermore, that when instituting or improving procedures for working with goals, in line with the suggestions in this chapter, it is best to move very gradually. It might even be best to first set just one or two goals with each staff member, and then to increase that number only after there is the competence and the mutual understanding between manager and staff member, that are essential to successful use of goals.

There are different types of goals. Very long-range goals (including mission statements for an organization) are implemented with shorter-range goals. Some organizations even differentiate between strategic goals and tactical (operational) goals, which support them. (Please remember that, despite some controversy on the definition of the two words, goals and objectives, they will be used interchangeably here, for the purposes of this book). Successful use depends on how well goals are set, communicated, and respected, and how well respective accountabilities are understood and acted on. Specific work on goals is done in action steps. (See Question 8.2e below)

At the highest organizational level, the very long-range goals are often referred to as 'vision', an important element of effective leadership. Vision is meaningless, however, unless it is shared, supported by relevant strategies (long-term goals), and accepted. While vision is usually considered to be the province of top management, one can talk about vision at the level of a small department. There it is likely to be the goal of the department's manager to make the unit a highly effective one. In reality, this vision shows itself in the form of specific long-term and short-term goals, in conformance with the goals at higher levels in the organization. One could even think of vision for individuals, in terms of their aspirations and their respective roles in the unit.

It is important to understand how goals are developed. When a large project is initiated, when a major opportunity is identified, or a major problem faces the organization, the general strategy for dealing with the situation is usually:

- For the highest level involved to decide on general approach and to set broad goals; work on these goals is then apportioned among the members of this level
- They, in turn, apportion their goals with subsidiary goals among the managers on their staff, with appropriate participation
- And so on, down the organization.

In this manner, each level assumes responsibility for its share of the entire project or problem and there is no need for 'micro-management' by higher levels.

Whether originated by the unit or organization manager, or based on suggestions by staff members, the specifics of what is to be accomplished with a goal, is most often part of the functional aspect of the goal decision or plan. It depends on the 'business' of the organizational unit (sales, marketing, health care, operations, government agency work, quality, investments, finance, etc.) How the specifics are to be decided, how various aspects of the subsidiary goals and goals for individuals are to be set, and how the goals are to be implemented, are the issues from the leadership-in-management perspective. These concern participation, coordination, communications, competencies, etc.—all the issues discussed in this book. As was pointed out before, the habit of thinking of a set of universally applicable questions with every decision/plan, will automatically consider both sets of issues, those which apply to the occupation and field/discipline in which the organization operates and those which apply everywhere—the leadership-in-management issues.

As mentioned before, goals are useful for the organization, the organizational unit, the team, and the individual. Goals for the organizational unit have to be set to help the organization achieve its goals; in a similar vein, goals of teams and individuals must be in line with those of the organizational unit. For that reason, managers of organizational units should participate as much as possible, when the organization's goals are set. Likewise, extensive participation by team leaders and/or individuals is likely to be beneficial in setting the unit's goals. Finally, team and individual goals are best set with extensive participation of the respective staff member(s). (For the specifics of participation, see Chapter 5)

Goals define what is to be accomplished by the person or group responsible for a goal, during the coming period. They address specific projects and should always include goals on improvement in central matters such as production, quality, financial matters, etc. Goals should be supported, at the level of the individual or team, by action steps that are most likely to achieve them. Goals should always be set jointly. With less experienced/mature staff members, even action steps should be discussed. (For the important distinction between goals and action steps, see Question 8.2e.)

When setting goals it is important to keep the 8-questions model in mind, in addition to the technical/functional issues. This is particularly relevant because the latter aspects are usually dominant and have a tendency to overshadow all other considerations.

The idea of working toward goals seems deceptively simple, yet much is involved. Specifically, the questions discussed below should be addressed if the goals program is to be successful.

When reading them, please keep in mind that they apply to goals for individuals every bit as much as to goals for teams, for larger organizational units, and for entire organizations. Use of an effective hierarchy of goals can help to ensure that all segments of an organization focus on the same results. For higher-level managers they provide an opportunity to ensure that the efforts of all segments of the organization and of all individuals will be coordinated toward the goals of the organizational unit or of the organization for which they are responsible. Please note that this careful wording applies to managers in charge of entire multi-national organizations as well as to the manufacturing director in a small company, the team manager who is responsible for the work of a small team, to the manager of a function to whom no one reports and even to someone who is only temporarily in a leadership position on a team or a project. With the appropriate use of goals there is little likelihood that managers will bypass lower level managers (to work directly with their staff members), or that staff members will go over the heads of the managers to whom they report.

QUESTIONS AND ISSUES FOR SUCCESSFUL USE OF GOALS (THESE WILL BE DISCUSSED IN CONSIDERABLE DETAIL AFTER THIS LISTING)

- Question 8.1—Should a Goal, or Goals, Be Set? Will the Challenge, Problem, or the Opportunity for Improvement (the desired outcome conditions) Be Met More Effectively if Goals are Used?
- Question 8.2—If Goals are Used, What Will Give Them High Quality? This Means:

  - Question 8.2a—Will the unit's goals lead to achievement of the desired outcome conditions (Are they in line with the larger organization's goals)?
  - Question 8.2b—Do the goals address matters that are important, rather than those that are urgent?
  - Question 8.2c—Are the goals both challenging and realistic (achievable)?
  - Question 8.2d—Are the goals specific enough, stating completion date, quantity, quality, and resources to be used (when not obvious), so it is possible to determine how well they were achieved (in other words, are they measurable)?
  - Question 8.2e—Are the goals 'true' goals or are they action steps?
  - Question 8.2f—Are the goals for a meaningful time span?
- Question 8.3—If Goals Are Used, What Other Issues Should Be Considered?
  - Question 8.3a—Are the goals being communicated effectively to all stakeholders?
  - Question 8.3b—Are there an appropriate number of goals for the organizational unit and for each staff member, considering staff abilities and workload?
  - Question 8.3c—Is there appropriate participation by stakeholders in the setting of the goals, including those that are for individuals?
  - Question 8.3d—Have you, the manager, accepted your respective share of responsibility for achievement of the goals?
  - Question 8.3e—Do goals address not only the functional achievements but also all the other management/leadership issues that affect work satisfaction and motivation, as well as competence of all involved managers, staff members and external stakeholders?
  - Question 8.3f.—Is the award/reward system of the organization coordinated with goal performance?

Question 8.1—Should a Goal, or Goals, be Set? Will the Challenge, Problem or Opportunity (Or the Desired Outcome Conditions for a Decision or Plan) be Met More Effectively if Goals are Used?

When a plan for a complex challenge, problem or opportunity is developed, it typically will consist of a large number of specific accomplishments. Most of the time it is not advisable to set goals for all of them, based on questions 8.2b and 8.3b. In these cases, a selection has to be made from the items in the plan—formal goals will be set at the outset on some and the others will be postponed or be handled like all other matters not covered by goals on which teams and individuals work. One major consideration for selecting the items on which to set goals, is the possible need for coordination between departments. A major benefit of goals, after all, is the more focused communication that they bring. For goals that require coordination between teams or departments, and even between individuals, the detailed specification of what is to be accomplished, the need to develop subsidiary goals or action steps for all individuals and teams involved, the timelines for these steps and for the goal itself, all contribute to the greater likelihood that work will proceed smoothly.

One other thought that helps to select which items should be covered with goals is the extent to which the goal achievement can be expressed so it will be possible to determine whether, or how well, it was achieved (see Question 8.2d). If either required resources or the time when the goal would have to be reached cannot be determined at the outset, then action steps have to define, at least temporarily, what is to be accomplished. A formal goal can be set later, when more is known about some uncertainties, such as the influences of external factors.

It should also be kept in mind that the process of determining goals, deciding on plans, or on results to be achieved, is not a one-step process. Some desired results or outcomes are immediately apparent when a situation presents itself. Others may come into view during discussions about what will be done, and/or as work begins or progresses. The goals and tasks that become apparent at the outset of the planning process, those that flow directly from the desired outcome conditions, could be considered as tentative. Then, after some participation, and brief thought to the remaining ones of the eight questions, they might be modified and/or augmented. Some of these may not be for managers or staff members in the department with primary responsibility for the outcome. They may require consultation and coordination with other departments.

One of the incidental benefits of applying the Eight-Questions Model is that it brings early thought about other results that may be desirable. Backtracking or duplication of effort during implementation may therefore be avoided. In fact, the entire planning process is an iterative one in which desired outcome conditions, goals, and the Eight Questions Model, interact to define the best way to go. This will happen automatically as the habit of using the model takes hold.

Question 8.2—If Goals Are Used, What Will Give Them High Quality?

Several issues are involved here, as discussed in Questions 8.2a through 8.2f below. Most of these issues apply to plans even if formal goals are not used.

Question 8.2a—Will the Goals Lead to Achievement of the Desired Outcome Conditions or Improvement? (Are they in line with the larger organization's goals)?

Goals of an individual and/or of a team or an organizational unit are of good quality only if they are in line with, and contribute to the larger organization's goals (and/or bring improvement that is also in line with its interests/goals).

Question 8.2b—Do the Goals Address Matters That are Important, Rather Than Those That are Urgent?

Goals are useful only if they focus on achievements pertaining to a major project or to some significant improvement. This is equally true for individual goals as it is for team and departmental goals. If goals are set on trivial matters, they are not likely to earn the respect of the staff, nor do they help to separate important matters from unimportant ones. Goals are most useful if they are used to focus attention on continuing improvement—on identifying what will be most helpful for this purpose, on the specific changes that would do most good—and then to serve as guides to their achievement.

One of the significant benefits of goals is that they can assure that the matters on which they are set, receive their proper share of attention in relation to more urgent ones, because goals have time-targets that slot them into a work schedule.

The relative importance and urgency of something to be achieved, can help determine whether it deserves a goal. A diagram first published in a simulation exercise (Didactic Systems, 1977a), then in other Didactic Systems publications, and made famous in two of Stephen Covey's books (1989, 1994), can shed some light on how these two characteristics of a project apply to goal setting. *Urgency* refers to the need for rapid action, while *importance* concerns significance to broader accomplishments and interests of the goal-setter or to the organization. Considering the four possible combinations of these two considerations, surprisingly, it is not the important-and-urgent matters that deserve to be considered for goals—they automatically receive maximum immediate attention and it is too late to set goals on them. Matters that are important-and-not-urgent are the best candidates for goals. These matters include improvements in operations that will lead to better performance and greater achievement. They are also the ones that are often postponed repeatedly if they do not receive the attention that goals bring.

Goals bring with them time-posts for action steps or subsidiary goals and thus can ensure that these matters do not get pushed aside until they reach crisis stage. At that point it may be too late to deal with them most effectively—but being both urgent and important at that time, they will certainly receive maximum attention, the way battling the biting alligators always has priority over draining the swamp. Matters that are neither urgent nor important certainly do not need goals and those that are urgent but not important can be delegated to someone who has the time to do them quickly.

Unfortunately, important-but-not-urgent matters may not present themselves automatically. They are not current problems and therefore do not 'ring a bell' to demand attention. Very often they are derived from the manager's 'vision' of the role and desirable level of accomplishment for the unit.

Participation by staff members can frequently be useful to identify areas where opportunities for improvement may exist, and possibly even what modifications might be desirable for the 'vision'.

Important reminder: all goals, as stated earlier, concern important matters. Therefore, appropriate participation by staff members is essential when setting goals for the organizational unit, with and for the team, and with and for a staff member. In situations, when a staff member needs help in setting the action steps to work toward a goal, the appropriate participation principles, of course, also apply there. (see Chapter 5)

Question 8.2c—Are the Goals Both Challenging and Realistic (Achievable)?

According to much of what has been published on the subject, goals can have a high motivational impact on the organizational unit as well as on individuals, if they are challenging and realistic. Realistic means that they are believed to be achievable. In practice it does not necessarily work out that way, partly because there is a contradiction here: 'realistic/achievable' means that the goal can be reached. Yet, 'challenging' means that, even with intelligently applied high-level effort, matters beyond the control of the individual and of the organizational unit can prevent the goal from being fully satisfied.

All goals are predictions of what can be achieved with diligence and maximum reasonable effort. To determine what the goal will require in the way of budget and time, and any quantities that may be involved, requires some form of forecasting. Therefore, if a goal is to be set both challenging and fully realistic, and those who set the goal are very good at their craft and at forecasting, then it is likely that 50 percent of the goals will be achieved earlier or will be over-achieved and 50 percent of the goals will be achieved late, more resources may be needed, or there will be a shortfall in quantity or quality. Perfect achievement of a goal occurs most rarely, in the sense that budget, quantity, quality, completion time, and any other conditions are met exactly. Still, the best goals are those that are challenging, and realistic/achievable. To determine what will make a goal realistic, it is often necessary to lay out the steps that could be taken to achieve the goal. A goal that is suggested by the manager, or is set with extensive involvement of the staff, usually requires a review of the alternative steps needed to reach it (plan alternatives). Without such planning a goal is more of a guess than a serious effort to provide meaningful direction for the team, staff, or individual.

It may sometimes be better not to insist on specifics for a goal. Instead, the goal can temporarily be defined by the action steps that define the *what, when,* and the *how* of the plan to achieve it. Often this alternative is more useful than specifics, such as quantities, quality, and timelines for the goal, at least in the interim, until the view is clearer and specific attributes of the goal can be set. If the action steps are fully appropriate, and competently executed, the best possible outcome will be achieved.

Question 8.2d—Are the Goals Specific Enough so it is Possible to Determine How Well They Were Achieved (are they measurable)?

Often goals are too vaguely stated to be useful. However, a goals program that provides long-term goals as general guidance needs to support them with short-term goals. When desirable, all should be in writing. To be measurable, short-term goals must specify, as much as possible, quantity and quality of the end result (outcome), the resources that can be used (if not obvious) and, of course, the dates by when they are to be achieved. Longer-term goals need not be equally precise, as long as the short-term goals that will bring their achievement are indeed sufficiently specific.

Question 8.2e—Are the Goals True Goals or Are They Action Steps?

Useful goals are different from action steps. Though both should be arrived at with appropriate participation (extensive for goals, much less so for action steps), goals should be realistic and challenging. Action steps, of course, must also be realistic but they need not be challenging. Deciding on action steps is primarily the staff member's responsibility. The major distinction is that goals are end results that may be affected by matters outside the control of the person, team, department, or organization that is working to achieve them. By contrast, tasks that are not likely to be subject to interference by forces beyond the control of those who work on them, are action steps. This distinction is critical in determining who has responsibility and who should/could be held accountable.

To see clearly whether something is a goal or an action step, the question should be asked: "If that person/team/organization wants to achieve that result, can anything other than an emergency or some other major, totally unforeseeable event, stand in the way?" If the answer is "no", it is an action step and the staff member can be held accountable. In other words, if something can be accomplished with adequate, competent effort, than it is an action step and not a goal.

With an action step, which is basically a task or simple project, as manager, you do what you do with other day-to-day activities; you ensure that the staff member clearly understands what has to be done, and that he/she has the necessary competence and resources. You have entirely different tasks and responsibilities with respect to goals. With a goal you have to consider all the issues involved in making a goals program successful. You, and the staff member accepting the goal for himself/herself or on behalf of a team, both agree on a completion date and you follow up as indicated. For your role and responsibilities, see Question 8.3d below.

In other situations there may not be enough time to the completion date of the plan so that 'real' goals cannot realistically be set—see Question 8.2f below. In those situations, the Eight-Questions Model suggests that it is better to set action steps directly, rather than as elements leading to a goal.

Question 8.2f—Are the Goals for a Meaningful Time Span?

Setting goals properly may require considerable thought, and should involve timelines for the supporting action steps. As mentioned previously, it is therefore impractical to set them on urgent matters that have to be done in a few hours or days—urgent matters require immediate attention and setting milestones is usually not practical. When something is so important that it might be appropriate to set goals but there is not enough time, the action steps for the 'goal' to be achieved can be set instead.

An acronym is used widely to summarize many, but not all, of these features of goals—SMART:

- *S* is for Specific. Is there enough detail to ensure that what is to be accomplished is clear to everyone?
- *M* is for Measurable. How will you gauge progress, know when you are there?
- *A* is for Achievement-Oriented. Something meaningful is to be achieved, or accomplished.
- *R* is for Resources, or Realistic. What resources, in time, budget, and personnel, will be needed to accomplish the goal/objectives? And, is the goal Realistic? (As we have seen, a goal is realistic if it is achievable.)
- *T* is for Time-bound. By when is the goal to be achieved?

The important item not covered by SMART is the need for goals to be challenging.

Question 8.3—If Goals are Used, What Other Issues Should be Considered?

In addition to quality of goals issues (Questions 8.2a–8.2f), if goals are to be used, other questions (Question 8.3a–8.3f) deserve some thought.

Question 8.3a—Are the Goals Being Communicated Effectively to All Stakeholders?

Timely communications in appropriate forms with all stakeholders (staff, customers, suppliers, other departments, etc.), are of utmost importance in helping to ensure that everyone knows what is to be achieved and when, and what the respective roles are. Only with that knowledge can there be full coordination and cooperation. Sound communications contribute to a motivational climate for goal achievement and are important to ensure that stress related to the 'challenging' aspect of goals is held within reasonable limits. Even goals of individuals require communications—to all who might be expected to provide support and those who may be affected.

Question 8.3b—Are There an Appropriate Number of Goals for the Organizational Unit and for Each Staff Member, Considering Abilities and Workload?

There is no limit to the number of goals that could be set if goals were set on all the things an organizational unit and its people do. Still, an individual and a team can work on only a limited number of goals, since the regular, more routine work, cannot be neglected. It is therefore of utmost importance to be selective (to keep the guideline of important-but-not-urgent in mind, that automatically points to desirable improvements).

The current and anticipated workload, as well as the abilities of the individual staff member or team, are the primary influences on the number of goals that can, or should, be set. Organizational and individual goals should therefore be set only to ensure progress on major projects and on those end results that are most important to the performance of the individual or of the organizational unit. The latter are usually matters that pertain to some form of desirable improvement. The special attention that goals bring helps to ensure that these matters will be given adequate priority.

All staff members have to understand, of course, that everything not covered by goals—all regular work—shall be done at least as well as in the past. One could even consider this statement as a goal that always applies.

Question 8.3c—Is There Appropriate Participation by Stakeholders in the Setting of the Goals?

Participation-in-decision-making concepts have to be observed throughout the goal setting process, and even during assignment of tasks or projects. Without appropriate participation, there is less of a motivational climate, and the image of the manager as an effective leader is reduced.

Question 8.3d.—Have you, the Manager, Accepted Your Respective Share of Responsibility for Achievement of the Goals?

It is not hard to see why goal setting has heavy impact on the performance of an organizational unit. However, goals can easily lead to political strategies. In an organization that has established a climate favorable to achievement, and where communications are open, it is likely to be safe for an organizational unit, as well as for an individual, to set and to shoot for challenging, ambitious goals. However, if the climate is such that negative consequences can result from failure to fully achieve a goal, then there is strong incentive for goal setters to gain acceptance of conservative, less challenging goals.

To ensure that the goals program adds to a positive climate, you as the manager, have to be involved, and be satisfied with the methods your staff uses to work toward accomplishment of their goals. You have to provide any support that may be needed, and, most important of all, you have to be prepared to accept your full share of responsibility for the outcome of the strategies.

Does that mean that, ultimately, you are responsible for all goals? Yes, that is exactly what it means.

Staff members of an effective leader/manager are held responsible for only two things:

- To set and accomplish ambitious action steps
- To notify the leader/manager immediately as soon as it becomes apparent that a goal is in jeopardy, so that the manager can decide whether to provide additional human or other resources, or change the goal.

Sometimes a staff member or lower level manager may have the responsibility to achieve a goal or task that requires a diverse, informal project team. The two responsibilities are the same for such a team leader, even when one or more of the team members are individuals from other departments who are at higher levels.

Fortunately what applies to you, also applies to the person to whom you report, that person's manager, and so on up the line. Every manager, up to but not including the top, also has the two obligations of staff members listed above—and not more. Where the organization does not embrace this thinking, you can still adhere by these guidelines. You will not be worse off, and probably in better position, when you make your staff aware that you see the respective responsibilities of managers and staff members, as suggested here. You thereby free them to set ambitious goals and they will let you know, in time, when they need your support because a goal may not be achieved without additional resources and/or your help. What goals you set for the team or department, depends on the way higher-level managers look at respective responsibilities.

Question 8.3e—Do Goals Address not Only the Functional Achievements but Also the Management/Leadership Aspects?

For the use of goals to be effective, goals have to address all relevant issues. This means that all eight questions in the model need attention when a goal is set. Goals should consider any competence needs that may exist and either include whatever competence development may be necessary, or trigger goals on such improvement. It may be equally appropriate to consider a goal or goals pertaining to matters that affect the satisfaction of staff members, when goals are set for a project or for improvement of an aspect of an organizational unit's work.

Question 8.3f—Is the Reward/Award System of the Organization Coordinated With Goal Performance?

It is highly desirable, of course, for people to be rewarded fairly. A staff member's record pertaining to setting of challenging goals, and the effort to achieve them, should therefore reflect themselves in the performance evaluation and through them to the rewards that the staff member receives. These include psychological rewards and concern for excessive stress, semi- and fully tangible rewards (compensation, benefits and bonuses) and consideration for promotional and developmental assignment opportunities).

By accepting your share of responsibilities, and by making most effective use of the organization's reward system for thought and effort with respect to goals, you can help ensure that there is a motivational climate for setting and achieving of challenging goals.

DELEGATION, GOALS AND PARTICIPATION

Delegation is intimately connected to goals and participation. A brief discussion of delegation can therefore serve as a conclusion and as reinforcement of this and some of the preceding topics.

Managers delegate when their own workload threatens to require more time than they have available. They usually think of delegation in general terms without distinguishing whether they are 'delegating' goals or action steps (tasks). Yet there is a distinction here.

Delegating projects will usually involve setting of goals and require thought of all the questions and issues that were discussed in this chapter and of those that are covered in Chapter 5.

However, tasks (some of the manager's own action steps or part of the regular duties) can also be "delegated"—or assigned. Appropriate selection of the individual to whom to assign a task is necessary, of course. There is also a need for participation in specifically defining the limits of the task and of the resources that may be used, including any support the manager may have to provide. The assignee can then be expected to fully complete the task and responsibility is entirely the staff member's.

Sometimes an assignment delegated to a staff member requires the efforts of several staff members at the same organizational level, and possibly even staff members from different departments. In these situations it is even more important, than with projects delegated to individuals, to clearly define the limits of the staff member's authority, and the responsibilities of the respective individuals. Mutual understanding on when the manager has to be asked for support and/or involvement is most essential in these situations.

A BRIEF REVIEW OF WHAT HAS BEEN DISCUSSED SO FAR

It may be useful at this point, before revisiting the scenario analysis from Chapter 3, to focus on the core of what has been covered in the preceding chapters.

Every decision and plan requires consideration of all relevant issues, the non-technical ones, and the technical ones (the latter are not discussed in this book—issues and quality criteria for them are provided in the literature and educational programs of the respective field or discipline.). To achieve high quality for a decision or plan, there has to be careful attention to detail—to all the relevant issues (of both types).

In some chapters two separate types of topics were discussed: a) the questions for the non-technical issues, and b) skills relevant to implementation of aspects of the topic. It is important to distinguish these two clearly since the primary objective of this book is to help readers gain insight into a process that has, as its foundation, the Eight-Questions Model. Providing ideas for sharpening skills is entirely secondary to this objective.

The questions and subsidiary questions that could be used have been identified and described in Chapters 4 through 10, and in this chapter. None are meant to be final arrangements. They are offered primarily as a foundation on which readers can build their own thorough system. However, such a system should be intended to satisfy all the responsibilities of a manager, as is attempted here. It should also be universally applicable, comprehensive, actionable, and based on past research on motivation, management, leadership, and decision-making as reported in the literature.

The conclusion of the discussion so far is that managers will achieve the highest possible levels of success if they develop the habit to apply a set of appropriate questions, such as the 8-Questions Model, in the standard decision-making steps.

APPENDIX TO CHAPTER 11
MORE DETAIL FOR THE ANALYSIS OF THE HELP DESK SCENARIO FROM CHAPTER 3

This revisit of the analysis of the scenario in Chapter 3 is intended to show how the greater knowledge of the eight questions can expand on the issues that can be considered. Chapter 3 has shown that decisions and plans can be improved even with only a broad-brush analysis based on a list of the Eight-Questions Model and on prior experience, but without exposure to the subsidiary questions and their issues that deserve consideration. The outcome most likely will include more beneficial features than it would have without the thought discipline that reviewing the list had imposed. As this appendix will show, more depth of knowledge of the issues that lie behind the questions, can further enhance thoroughness and quality of the analysis.[2]

Rather than repeat the analysis from Chapter 3, this appendix merely introduces additional thoughts that might not have been considered with-

---

2. As already pointed out in Chapter 3, when tentatively identifying the desirable outcome elements, and deciding on plans or goal areas and goals, there are five groups of issues to consider:
   - The technical/functional issues
   - The communications needs of the situation
   - Issues to ensure that the necessary and desirable competencies will be available where needed
   - Issues related to ensuring that stakeholder satisfaction will be as high as possible, but definitely not so low as to create obstacles
   - Issues related to appropriate participation

   Please note the extensive attention to communications, competence, satisfaction, and participation. As previously pointed out (Chapter 3), most people, and especially those with experience, can easily identify many of the technical/functional things that should be considered for action. It is the other four, the communications, competence, satisfaction, and participation issues that are often either neglected or ignored. A major benefit of the use of a comprehensive sound model, such as the Eight-Questions Model, is to help decision makers and planners think of these latter issues and give them equal attention so the process will be more comprehensive and thus of higher quality, at least from the leadership perspective.

out the information in Chapters 4 through 11, and adds any considerations that were not in the initial analysis. It also expands the analysis beyond decision process Steps 1 through 3 with a brief discussion of Steps 4 through 8.

Little needs to be added to Steps 1 and 2. The desired outcome conditions (Step1) were as apparent from the listing of the key words and abbreviated question statements, as they are with greater depth of knowledge. The same is essentially true of the assessment of relevance in Step 2, except that Communications, Competence, Satisfaction, and Progress Reviews, might now be given greater relevance than just 'somewhat'.

Step 3

Review of each one of the *relevant* questions (participation, communications, competence and satisfaction questions would always be relevant) to identify what insights they may bring, including possible revision of the desired outcome conditions.

Step 4

Identification of alternatives for addressing the problems, opportunities and challenges. It is useful to see that this step involves the eight questions because in most decisions there are many aspects to each alternative. Keeping the eight questions in mind helps to ensure that all useful aspects are considered.

Step 5

Collection of any information that is not yet available but might be needed or desirable. With that information, additional alternatives, and possibly also changes to the desired outcome conditions may become apparent, or existing ones be revised.

Step 6

Evaluation of the alternative plans resulting from the preceding steps in preparation for selecting the preferred one. This step applies the information (factual data), that may be available from Step 5, possibly with the use of decision support systems, as well as the 'common sense (intuitive or emotional inputs) of the decision maker(s) or planner(s), and the reversibility concept, in the evaluation. The preferred alternative should satisfy all aspects of the relevant questions which deserve some form of action, and, of course, also the desired outcome conditions.

Here, too, the eight questions have similar use as in Step 4. Like Step 2, this step may reveal matters that might be worth adding to the desired outcome.

Step 7

Review, and possibly revision of the elements of a desirable outcome, and *selection of the most desirable alternative* (its components). The eight questions apply here too.

Step 8

Implementation of the various aspects of the decision or plan, which means that, with appropriate participation, the goals would be apportioned to the teams and individuals who would then work on them. This step also requires monitoring to see whether the chosen alternative will, indeed, bring the desired outcome, and implementation revisions if obstacles have developed.

To avoid the need to refer back to Chapter 3, all steps will be discussed briefly here.

Step 1

In Step 1 the following preliminary elements of a desired outcome were identified:

- Revised tape message that overcomes the problems with the existing one
- Faster tech support response
- Optimum staffing level
- High level help desk staff and manager competence
- At least adequate satisfaction of all stakeholders (staff, customers, suppliers, other departments, etc.)
- Ensuring adequate communication of decisions and steps to all those who should be kept informed.

Step 2

In Step 2, only two questions were considered only somewhat relevant–norms and reviews. Based on the more detailed look at the questions, these two could be upgraded to relevant.

Step 3

For Step 3 it is now necessary to look at all the questions in detail.

Communications. Little needs to be added to the discussion in Chapter 3, except that the Vice President, if he or she became involved here or in the questions discussed later, would be concerned, if at all, only in ensuring, through channels, that all managers assume responsibility to see to it that communications satisfy all five subsidiary questions (1.1–1.5).

Participation. Here too, little needs to be added to the discussion of participation in Chapter 3 except to stress, again, that *all* team and individual goals or plan segments should be decided on with appropriate participation. Participation also needs to be considered with the resolution of all obstacles that may emerge. As was stated in Chapter 3, it is important to see that, in effect, the VP has delegated effectively to other managers. Thereafter the VP's role is primarily confined to providing any support they may need. The individual managers, of course, need to practice participation as outlined in Chapter 5.

Competence, Learning, and Selection, and the Satisfaction Questions. The coverage of these two questions was the same in Chapter 3 as it would likely be if the person analyzing the hypothetical scenario had more thorough knowledge of the leadership-in-management issues. However, competence considerations are certainly relevant, since the procedure changes and the potential accompanying stress require thought about effective competence enhancement. The same is true of satisfaction considerations, especially those covered by the first three questions (4.1-4.3). The changes that will undoubtedly be made should be arranged so that they do not bring significant stress, or resentment that might work against their effective implementation. Obviously a manager with both, thorough knowledge of leadership-in-management issues *and* in-depth knowledge of the situation is likely to see more specifics with respect to the things to consider.

Nothing in the scenario indicates that attention will be given to providing acknowledgement of staff member contributions through signs of appreciation for their respective contributions and through consideration of tangible rewards. Neither is there any mention of manager development for providing such signs. The discussion in Chapter 3 does touch on these issues and therefore is adequately complete.

Progress and Performance Reviews, and Performance Evaluations. In light of the lack of information about existing policies and procedures pertaining to these reviews and to performance evaluations, nothing can be added at this point, except to stress, that justice and fairness are key to these procedures if they are to bring beneficial, rather than detrimental results. However, this question, and especially procedures for progress reviews, should be considered as relevant in light of the many possible projects that will be worked on.

Coordination, Cooperation, and Conflict. Here too, the analysis in Chapter 3 was almost as sound as could be done with greater knowledge of the underlying issues, with one major exception as discussed in Chapter 9. It pertains to the need for effective procedures, because they are needed for good coordination. This is especially relevant when there are changes in the way work is to be performed such as in the case of a possible redesign of work flow in the department with specialization of some tech staff members, as mentioned in the analysis. It is important to remember that this question applies to the way coordination, as well as cooperation with people, procedures and especially with change, can be assured, while potentially damaging conflicts/disputes are prevented or resolved.

Cooperation challenges may also have to be considered if there is reason to anticipate conflicts and cooperation problems between people or with new procedures.

Norms, Ethics, Positive Discipline, Counseling. The discussion of this question is adequate in Chapter 3, and little if anything can be added with somewhat greater acquaintance with the eight questions.

Goals and Plans. The most significant change in the way the scenario is analyzed on the basis of greater awareness of the eight questions is treatment of goals and plans. Some of the outcome aspects that need to be satisfied to fully meet the challenges inherent in a situation may not call for goals, but may either require just action steps (see Chapter 11 for the distinction) or be so urgent as to require immediate attention. The situation in the scenario is not an emergency and the problem, while deserving immediate attention, does allow for the setting of goals or of carefully prepared plans. Most of the necessary action steps can be performed in working toward achievement of these goals or implementation of the plans.

In the example scenario of the high tech company, as in any real situation, the issues pertaining to goals (see Chapter 11), as stated repeatedly, apply not only to the highest level manager, the Vice President in this case, but to every manager and staff member who is involved with one of the projects generated by the challenges inherent in the scenario. The issues may even have significance and impact for individuals who are not involved in the projects but affected by them.

In Chapter 3, general areas for goals based on the identified desired outcome conditions were listed. However, the goals and tasks that become apparent at the outset of the analysis process, those that flow directly from the desired outcome conditions, could be considered as preliminary, or temporary. Then, after some participation, and brief thought to the other questions, they, as well as the desired outcome conditions might be augmented with revisions in the outcome conditions, and with additional goals and tasks in later steps of the decision making process. Some of the goals or desirable/necessary actions may be for managers or staff members in the Sales and Marketing Department. The latter may require consultation and coordination with the respective other Department, or possibly even with the President. In the scenario the technical/functional areas immediately apparent for goals or actions appropriate for the respective teams, and/or for individuals, were listed as:

- Preparation and approval of a script, for a satisfactory tape message
- Preparation of a computer program for implementing the message so it will give accurate information to callers
- Recording of the tape message and testing it in conjunction with the program
- Determination and implementation of optimum staffing for the faster tech support response including evaluation of feasibility of flexible staffing, possibly with use of some-part-time employees and/or staff members from other departments, during peak demand periods
- Investigation of possible use of specialized teams

In addition, the leadership goals triggered by a quick review of the 8-Questions model were on:

- Analysis of staff and manager competence strengths and deficiencies
- What should be done, if anything to enhance staff and manager competence
- Identification of possible programs to ensure satisfaction of staff and other stakeholders
- What should be communicated to the various departments of the company

As was to be expected, this list of goal areas is quite complete, since it was assumed that the Vice President was aware of the Eight-Questions model.

However, a review based on more detailed knowledge of the first four of the questions does expand the list a little and thus shows the benefit of the disciplined decision-making process. Specifically, the following leadership issues deserve further consideration:

- Identification of learning needs for individual managers and staff members in all departments affected by any changes that will take place
- Determination of delivery methods (for the necessary learning), and post-learning evaluation of competence
- Matters pertaining to most effective use of competence strengths
- Clarification that manager competence development should include development of competence in applying the 8-Questions model
- Establishing criteria for selection of staff members for teams and projects, and of new employees in light of the contemplated new procedures
- Establishing a stress monitoring process and procedures to adjust stress levels when desirable

There is also a need to set priorities on all these goals after they have been accepted by the various departments that would work on them, so that the more important ones would be worked on first.

Other issues raised by the remaining questions. Thought of goals or actions might arise when the other questions are reviewed, especially those that concern coordination, cooperation, positive discipline, progress/performance reviews, and tangible rewards. New ideas for goals that should be considered are likely to also come up during the definition and evaluation of alternatives.

Participation in the determination of goals might also have sharpened some initial primarily technical/functional goal areas with issues such as

- Changes in tech support procedures and cooperation with them
- Improved approaches to monitoring quality of activities, etc. as indicated below.
- Investigation, and possible use of alternative media channels for providing help, that are not currently in use, including web-site help service, e-mail, automated responses to frequently asked questions, fax-on-demand, and possibly others that new technologies would make available. These were mentioned under coordination but did not result in awareness that they were potential areas for one or more goals

In addition to identifying goal areas, the subsidiary questions of Question 8 pertain to quality of goals. This example of an analysis therefore would not be complete without preparing at least one specific goal. The goal has to be measurable, so that it is possible to determine how well it was achieved. In an analysis of a hypothetical situation, it is, of course, impossible to determine whether such a goal is achievable, and/or challenging. A specific example to show what a complete (high quality) goal might be like (whether written or communicated verbally), could be:

> By (date) specifications for a revised tape message shall be available. This message shall have been approved by the Customer Service Manager, the Director of Marketing, the Director of IS/IT, and the Vice President of Sales and Marketing.

Please note that this goal has a completion date, and specific quality requirements. These specifications make it possible to measure how well the goal has been achieved. The goal does not include words about any limitations on resources that may be used since none are required, other than the time of the person who has accepted assignment of this goal, and possibly some review time by those who have to approve it. These resource requirements are obvious from the wording of the goal and need not be spelled out separately.

When deciding what goals are appropriate to set, thought has to be given to the possible urgency of the result to be achieved, and the number of goals on which an individual or a team can work on effectively, as well as the other thoughts in Chapter 11. At least those goals (and results from plan segments) that are to be delegated, need to be stated so that the extent of accomplishment can be measured. Each of the possible goals referred to above would have to include, as much and as precisely as possible, any relevant quantities, measures of quality, and the *date* when it would have to be accomplished. It should also identify the resources that can be used (see discussion of this issue in Chapter 11).

With respect to delegation, more needs to be known about the situation before it is possible to determine which individuals or task-force teams might be considered for delegation of the various goals.

Before closing this analysis, a reminder: It would have been necessary to think of the guidelines several times during the incident, and afterwards, to come up with the thoughts discussed above. That is because the scenario described a large number of decisions. Though the guidelines should be considered several times, only very few are likely to be relevant after the first review. Still, there is benefit to giving fleeting thought to guidelines that are not relevant to the situation itself—they may trigger useful thoughts of matters to consider after the challenge or problem has been resolved.

Decision Steps 4 through 8

These steps were not covered in Chapter 3 and therefore they are briefly discussed here.

Step 4

Identification of alternatives for addressing the problems, opportunities and challenges.

Once the initial evaluation of the relevance of the eight questions and the results of a preliminary review of the questions has been completed, it is possible to decide on initial alternatives that satisfy all eight questions. These are complex alternatives, of course, since each one has many features.

Basic components of the various alternatives that could be identified, without knowledge of the history of decisions/plans that may have dealt with them and without information about suggestions that would be made by participants, could consist of some or all of the following:

- Revising the tape
- Creating a system of internal and external part-time staff additions for peak periods
- Creating a system of specialists
- Adding other media channels for providing help, that are not currently in use, such as web site help service with automated responses to frequently asked questions, fax-on-demand, e-mail, etc.
- Various forms of staff and manager training programs
- Various options for enhancing communications
- Various approaches to meeting satisfaction needs of staff (and possibly of other stakeholders)
- Etc.

Some of these are likely to emerge only if some or all of the eight questions (or a similar set) were asked. That is particularly the case with respect to the last three in the list above. All, or most of these elements of possible alternatives could be combined in several realistic arrangements to create a limited number of concrete initial options from which the most desirable one could be selected in Step 7.

Step 5

Collection of any information that is not yet available yet might be needed or desirable.

This search for information that would be useful for evaluating the identified alternatives would be based on the data/information needs of the technical issues and those of the eight leadership-in-management questions. As the information is collected, additional alternatives may become apparent or it may become desirable to modify existing ones. Because this information can be obtained only in a real situation, and not in a hypothetical one, very little can be said about this fifth step, and the following ones in this scenario. It should be obvious, however, that information pertaining to steps that might be considered for enhancing competence (including the types of training programs that might be desirable), ensuring that communications are as complete and effective as possible, and bringing the highest possible satisfaction of staff members, might not be sought if the eight questions were not asked.

Step 6

Evaluation of the alternatives in preparation for selecting the preferred one.

In this step, the alternatives are evaluated with the use of additional information that may have been obtained, on the basis of the technical issues that apply and on the basis of the extent to which they satisfy the relevant ones of the eight leadership-in-management questions. The preferred alternative should, of course, be the one that best satisfies all these considerations as well as the desired outcome conditions.

Step 7

Review, and possibly revision, of the elements of a desirable outcome, and selection of the most desirable alternative (its components, and considering reversibility where possible).

This decision step, would only apply if the evaluation of alternatives uncovers one or more items that would enhance the desirable outcome conditions. After the identification of such items, Steps 5 and 6 would be repeated.

Step 8

Implementation of the various aspects of the decision or plan. During implementation, with appropriate participation, the goals would be apportioned to the teams and individuals who would then work on them. Consideration of the 8 questions is likely to enhance the quality of the effort. This step also requires monitoring to see whether the chosen alternative will, indeed, bring the desired outcome, and implementation revisions, if obstacles have developed.

This step is likely to achieve the desired outcome conditions and also point the way to resolving some indirectly related inadequacies in the organization's operation.

Conclusion

As this analysis has shown, enhanced knowledge of questions, those provided in this book or equivalent ones, is likely to bring more thorough decisions and plans than would be possible without them.

Though the process appears complicated and time consuming when in written form, once a leader/manager has acquired the habit to use it, very little time is needed. In many cases it can be completed within a few moments and possibly even save time, as pointed out previously (see Analysis Procedure in Chapter 3).

As pointed out in the *Concluding Thoughts* of Chapter 3, practice will build this habit and it, in turn, will make the process easy and rapid. Furthermore, some, and possibly many of the thoughts expressed above, might be superfluous since they could have been raised in previous decisions and steps will already be in place to meet and possibly eliminate those challenges.

CHAPTER 12

APPLICATION OF THE EIGHT-QUESTIONS MODEL

INTERRELATIONSHIPS BETWEEN THE ISSUES COVERED BY THE MODEL

For a thorough understanding of the 8-Questions model, it is important to see clearly how the different groups of issues covered by the questions relate to each other. As has been mentioned previously, there is considerable overlap and mutual reinforcement. A few examples might be useful to clarify this point. The discussion below is not meant to be exhaustive, but merely to point to some of the interdependencies of the model's elements.

1. Impact of participation on the issues in other questions

    (a) Impact of Participation on Communications

    Involvement of staff members and others in strategy matters pertaining to communications is necessary only occasionally—when delicate issues are involved or when there is a need to communicate to many people. In those situations a manager might consider involving senior staff members with the what, how and when to communicate. Astute managers may also ask for comments from staff members to develop stronger bonds by providing evidence of their regard for the staff member's opinions.

    However participation is at the core of open, two-way communications. When there is such communications, one-on-one, or face-to-face, or even in meetings, there are fewer misunder-

Planning, Common Sense, and Superior Performance, pages 129–136

standings, fewer errors are likely, and grievances come to the table earlier when they can be addressed more easily. Possibly even more important, participation can be used to make many messages more effective by asking for comments, questions, or suggestions, instead of merely providing information.

(b) Impact of Participation on Competence

Individuals know best what they know. However, they do not necessarily know what they do not know. Hence it takes at least two people to develop a thorough learning plan. Usually the manager takes the initiative and invites the staff member to assume a major role in deciding on the what-and-how of the most useful learning, by contributing her/his perspective on learning needs. Staff member and Human Resources participation in deciding on learning needs and approaches for groups of staff members will also bring better decisions and plans on these.

(c) Impact of Participation (including participation in communications) on Satisfaction

The impact of appropriate participation, combined with communications, on satisfaction cannot be overstated. It satisfies almost all the items listed in Question 4.3, by ensuring that staff members have more 'say', probably at an earlier time, more information about what is going on, more freedom to do the job as they want to do it, more guidance when they want or need it, more honest feedback on performance with recognition for accomplishments, more support when needed and probably also less over-the-shoulder looking, more interesting assignments, more knowledge by the manager (or supervisor) about their contributions, and with that, more confidence in their abilities.

Overall, these specific benefits of appropriate participation are likely to have strong positive effects in satisfaction for most if not all staff members. They bring stronger feelings of security, greater levels of trust with enhanced feeling of belonging, and higher levels of esteem. All this brings tighter bonds between staff member, manager, the organizational unit and even the entire organization.

(d) Impact of Participation on Progress and Performance Reviews and Performance Evaluations

Progress and performance reviews that are based primarily on the manager's views are symptoms of autocratic styles that violate much of what is discussed in this book. In both reviews it is the staff member, or lower level manager who should have the primary responsibility for decisions about actions that should be considered, by describing what has happened in the past, and by identifying corrective actions where desirable. With appropriate participation and communications, the manager's role then is essentially to discuss support that may be needed, to guide, and to counsel.

Performance evaluation is somewhat similar. Here the manager does have the autocratic responsibility to assess and compare against standards and performance of other staff members, based on the information that was obtained in the highly participative and fairly frequent reviews. Still, the primary emphasis should be on development of a competence and performance improvement plan that will lead to better evaluations the next time. For that plan the staff member, again, is in the lead with the manager's role the same as in the reviews.

(e) Impact of Participation on Coordination, Cooperation and Conflict

With appropriate participation, coordination obstacles come to light sooner, and can be addressed better, with input from the people who are on the firing line and are therefore likely to know best. Furthermore, with the enhanced job satisfaction and the more open communications that participation brings, there is a sounder foundation for thorough cooperation and earlier, more effective resolution of potentially damaging conflicts/disputes.

(f) Impact of Participation on Norms, Ethics, Organizational Justice, Positive Discipline, and Counseling

Participation impacts on the issues in this Question in many ways. Norms can and will be identified more accurately and earlier, as well as any changes that may be desirable. There is a better climate for the self-imposed positive discipline. Furthermore, with the greater mutual trust and open communications that appropriate participation stimulates, performance counseling can be far more effective. Even counseling on personal problems and on career direction is likely to be better. In addition, perceptions of inadequacies in organizational justice are likely to emerge so they can be worked on.

(g) Impact of Participation on Goals, Action Steps and Delegation

Thinking of the issues in Participation reminds the manager or project leader of the need to decide whom to invite to help set team and individual staff member goals or plans to set, or at least who should be kept abreast of developments. Asking people with technical knowledge, and those with awareness of the views of others, to participate in goal setting is likely to enhance the goals that will be set. Possibly most important, it gives the appropriate people a stake in the goals. It also reminds of the need to let people decide their own goals and especially their action steps as much as possible since interference may be perceived as micro-managing. Finally, with respect to delegating it reminds of the need to allow as much freedom to the delegatee to perform the delegated projects independently and to do whatever is necessary so the delegator will stay informed of progress.

2. Impact of the issues in other questions, on each other.

   A similar analysis of the impact of the issues in each question, on the issues in all other seven questions can be done. It should be obvious that nothing occurs without communications, that competence is involved in everything that is done, that the level of staff satisfaction affects all activities, that coordination, cooperation and conflict have pervasive impact, and so on. The only group of issues for which it might be difficult to show impact on the issues in other questions is the one that pertains to goals. Goals can and do impact everywhere, but they need not be formal goals. The issues pertaining to quality of goals are therefore only tangentially applicable. What makes goals effective, however, such as the number of goals, participation in setting them, communications, and the managerial responsibilities with respect to accomplishment of goals, do have broad impact on the other questions—whether formal goals are set whether they are, in effect, hidden in plans, or whether they are perceived to be part of the regular work.

OPPORTUNITIES, CHALLENGES AND PROBLEMS

Understanding the distinction between these three aspects of work, is useful here.

In general, problems present themselves and must be dealt with. Something is not as it should be and therefore corrective action is required.

The situation is often different with challenges and definitely so with opportunities. The work itself always brings challenges—matters that require competent approaches. Every situation might bring one or several challenges. That is why most decisions and plans lead to one or more others that also have to be considered.

Opportunities are different from problems and routine challenges that areconnected with a project or activity. They rarely ring bells the way problems do and they are not as easy to see as most challenges. It takes a different mindset to uncover opportunities to improve things, to find new products, to see business possibilities, to recognize the benefits of new arrangements, even the potential gain from taking a proactive, or unique stance on an issue. Opportunities usually represent long-term issues and require extra effort to see in a situation.

CHALLENGES RELATED TO THE SITUATION

If you have to deal with a situation that presents itself to you, you can quickly think of those of the eight questions that appear directly relevant, and follow the direction in which they lead.. Your decision or plan will be of high quality because you will have considered all or most of the technical and leadership-in-management issues that affect the choice of alternatives. However, it will not be as comprehensive as if you take another step—to consider related issues.

Very often a problem or challenge does not concern an isolated situation. It contains hints to other matters that might be worth a closer look. Among these might be underlying causes that bring the need for similar actions from time to time. Or they might be matters that, if left alone, could result in problems at a later date. For example, that might be the case of quality or conflict situations when the resolution might be only a temporary fix. Challenges inherent in a situation, that are initially hinted at by assessment of the eight questions for relevance, may be ignored even though they deserve closer examination. The example in Chapter 3 shows how the process leads to identification of other such matters that deserve some thought.

Some situations present several challenges—often both short-term and long-term ones. Complex situations usually do. When that is the case, they can sometimes all be resolved with one analysis using the 8 Questions. Sometimes two or more separate analyses may be needed.

USING A SYSTEM TO HELP REMEMBER ALL EIGHT BASIC QUESTIONS AND THEIR SUBSIDIARY QUESTIONS

Books that presented the same concepts as expressed here, described a model that can be helpful in remembering the questions (Rausch 1978/1985; Rausch & Washbush, 1998). The model was based on the fact that an organization will be as successful as possible if it has sound control over its direction, the competence to perform its tasks, and a satisfying climate. Because three words starting with C are involved, the model is called the 3Cs.

If you want to use a simple start for helping you remember the concepts in this book more easily, it might be useful for you to organize the eight questions into these three categories, though few fit neatly.

One possible arrangement for fitting the eight questions into the three categories, though certainly not the only one, could look like this:

Control could remind of :

- Participation
- Goals
- Coordination and cooperation
- Norms, ethics, positive discipline, and counseling
- Progress and performance reviews, and performance evaluations

Competence could remind of:

- Communications
- Recruiting and selection
- Competence strengths and competence development (management of learning, coaching, and on-the-job training)

Climate could trigger thoughts of:

- Psychological signs of appreciation
- Work-related stress
- Tangible and semi-tangible rewards
- Satisfaction of stakeholders other than staff members

The earlier books depicted two 3Cs diagrams, a basic and a comprehensive one. Both approaches, the one based on the 3Cs guidelines as well as the one based on the eight questions, are solidly based on the same past and current motivation and leadership research findings (see Chapter 14), and provide a practical vehicle for management and leadership decisions and plans. As a result of their comprehensive, yet flexible perspective, they can adapt easily to any situation, other cultures, and even to future research findings that may affect them.

Neither of the 3Cs diagrams, nor the Eight-Questions Model, have found widespread literature acceptance so far (though the diagrams have been used widely in the private and public sectors[1]). Critical and knowledgeable

---

1. The books have been the foundation for management development programs in the entire Federal Prison System, the training arms of the US Office of Personnel and the Alberta Government, JCPenney, the Girl Scouts, several hospitals, the American Management Associations, and many other lesser programs. The concept has been depicted in the West Point Academy's book on leadership, in Heyel's Encyclopedia of Management, in General Electric's summary handout to management learners at all levels, and is in continuing use for officer training in fire departments in many states.

readers have raised a few questions pertaining to the origin of the concept and to any support (empirical or in the literature) that serves to validate it. This chapter is not the place to respond to these questions. Still, they should be addressed in this book. Please refer to Section B in the Appendix, entitled "Validation Questions."

OTHER DECISION-MAKING ISSUES

There are three dimensions that contribute to the technical/functional aspects of decisions and plans that should be considered. They were briefly referred to in Chapter 1, under B. Strengths and limitations.

1. The first concerns the interpersonal *skills* important to implementation These knowledge/skill areas straddle technical/functional and leadership issues and include effectiveness in communicating, interviewing, coaching, counseling, resolving conflicts/disputes, participating in meetings or leading them, and similar activities. Only very few of these, the most relevant where something useful was added to the literature, were discussed here. The others are considered beyond the scope of this book and are either only mentioned or are touched on very lightly. It is beneficial to see that the discussions of these skills are not part of the focus of this book which concentrates on explanations of the eight questions that should be asked with every significant problem, challenge or opportunity.
2. Another dimension involves *financial matters*. Competent managers understand the financial/economic implications of their plans and actions. They can set up and work with budgets, and objectively evaluate alternatives in quantitative terms, such as costs, investment requirements, and expected returns. This dimension lies outside the scope of this book because it consists solely of technical issues, except to the extent to which it influences the identification of desired outcomes, and with it the setting of goals and the selection of participants for a decision/plan.
3. The third dimension is a *basic discipline*. It is theoretically possible for a manager to achieve excellent performance without competence in some basic discipline, such as computer science, selling, accounting, engineering, health care, law, or a craft. It is, however, unlikely that sustained high-level performance will be achieved without it. In our formal education and while gaining experience, we all learn at least one discipline in sufficient depth so we gain the respect of people as competent practitioners. As managers, and especially at higher levels, of course, we can no longer be expert, or even proficient in all

the functions under our jurisdiction. Still, even there we are likely to make better decisions, if we have practical expertise in a specific field, preferably in at least one of the major disciplines of the functional areas in which we are working. If not, it behooves us to devote the necessary effort to become familiar with the central one.

Sound foundation in a technical field, while not essential, can be helpful to establish and maintain a high regard of staff members (managerial and non-managerial) and associates, and for effective evaluation of reports or proposals submitted by technical specialists. Discussions of basic disciplines and specific fields are, of course, also beyond the scope of this book.

CHAPTER 13

APPLYING THE QUESTIONS

An Advanced Example Analysis (Steve's and Sally's Challenge—Planning for More Efficient Operations)

In this chapter a scenario is presented in greater detail to make it more realistic. Still, since it is hypothetical, it presents far less information than is available to the people in a real situation. Please note that the characters in the scenario are clearly competent managers. Still, their emphasis, as their past experience has prepared them, is heavily on the technical aspects of the challenges they face, and some of the leadership-in-management considerations are not adequately considered.

THE SCENARIO

A major mail order distributor of a broad line of health and beauty products regularly mails a catalog to customers and prospects. A questionnaire about the consumer's preferences is always included with the order form in the catalog. In some mailings small premiums are offered for return of the questionnaire. When questionnaires are received, the structured data (the checked items) is scanned into the computer for analysis and for later use in targeted promotions of specific product groups. The customer name, address, and other hand-written information are entered manually by staff-

---

Planning, Common Sense, and Superior Performance, pages 137–151

ers in the Data Input section that reports to Bill who, in turn, reports to the Operations Manager.

Steve, the IT/IS Manager who also reports to the Operations manager recently suggested that it might be profitable to upgrade the scanning program so it could also read the hand-written information. The Operations Manager liked the idea. It was discussed in a meeting of the managers reporting to him and Steve was asked to investigate it. If economically promising, Steve was to submit budget estimates for approval before proceeding with the project. Steve delegated the initial investigation to Sally, his MIS Systems manager.

Two weeks later Steve asked Sally to give him an update. "Did you get all the figures on the scanners and programming costs, and were you able to finish the forecast?" Steve got right to the point, even before Sally had time to sit down in the comfortable chair next to the little coffee table. "I certainly did." There was a hint of pride in Sally's tone. She continued, more hesitantly. "But, I am also quite concerned. We'll save some money alright, but the impact on our people, that's another story."

"What do you mean? I thought that our initial estimates showed that we would not have to cut staff—won't attrition and the growing workload take up most of the slack? Is that no longer true?"

"I'm afraid not. We may have been a little too conservative in estimating how many hours we will save with the scanners and the efficient program concept a consultant has shown me. Right after I met with her, I went through a bunch or incoming mail and made some specific realistic assumptions about the time it will take to scan the questionnaires, and about the proportion that would have to be entered manually. The good news is that, unless the people who will respond to our mailings with the new questionnaires, will mess up more extensively than I think they will, we'll be quite a bit more efficient than we had expected. The bad news is that we may have to lay off people after all.

I have spoken with Bill who is quite concerned and who is keeping the Operations Manager informed. We have jointly checked informally with Personnel. They don't think they can place any of the input people in other departments, though they'll try. There is a severance package they can offer to anyone who'll be laid off. They will tell people about that, and about any job openings for which they could apply. All that's useful but it doesn't really do much—it would have been great if they knew of jobs they could offer." Sally hesitated and then continued. " We've got to look at the staff and see who'll get hit. It's sad."

"OK. We'll have to do that." Steve agrees but returns to his main concern. "First, though, do you have the budget figures?"

"I have the capital budget requirements for this entire thing—equipment, the consultant fee for programming, piloting and debugging costs, and questionnaire design. I have also shown our regular equipment replacement needs so you can see the whole picture. Printing will be in the Public Relations and Marketing budgets. As far as our operating budget is concerned, I thought I would prepare that after I knew whether you want to move ahead full blast, or take a gradual approach."

"It's probably best to move as quickly as possible, considering the transition needs. Let' get it over with, so the agony will be short and so there will be no lingering concerns about job security by the staff that remains."

"I think you are right, Steve. I was leaning toward that myself. Ok. I'll have the operating budget figures for you tomorrow or the day after."

"That'll be fine. Now let me see what you did with the capital budget."

Steve was satisfied with what Sally showed him. "This looks fine. Thanks. I'll submit it as you've presented it here. Now, let's assume that we get approval. I am quite sure that will happen, especially since you expect even greater savings than we had anticipated. How do you plan to proceed then?"

"We could look at the projects that will have to be done. I could work up a tentative plan with goals for you to look at and then we could see how Operations, Marketing, Public Relations, and Personnel would feel about them. I'll work with Bill on this."

Steve thought that sounded good but he suggested that it might be useful if Sally first gave him a chance to look at what she was thinking, before she brought in Bill. They could then jointly decide which of the steps in the plan involved her and Bill, and which should be taken up with other people.

Sally agreed and promised to have the draft plan the next day.

By the end of the day, Sally was finished and took one more look at the steps she had listed:

1. Analyze the impact of the program to estimate how many staff members, and which ones, may have to be laid off
2. Jointly with Personnel, prepare and issue specific communications about the tentative plans, to the entire staff
3. Bill and someone from Personnel to speak with each staff member who might be affected, in individual meetings, to explain what might happen and how the company will provide help to hold hardship to a minimum.
4. Order one scanner
5. Finalize the questionnaire, jointly with Marketing and Public Relations
6. Authorize the consultant to proceed with program development
7. Arrange with Public Relations and Marketing to make a pilot mailing, as soon as the questionnaires are ready, and to prepare for a second one soon thereafter

8. Process half the returns from the first pilot mailing without any new equipment, entering the data into the data base by hand, as was done previously with the old questionnaire
9. As soon as the scanner and the new program are installed, test the program with the remaining returns from the first pilot mailing and compare with the manual entries; estimate the time savings that scanners will bring
10. Revise, and debug the program, as necessary
11. Make the second pilot mailing, use the scanner on the returns from that mailing and make any final adjustments that may be necessary
12. Arrange with Public Relations and Marketing to proceed with the new questionnaires on all future mailings
13. Purchase and install additional scanners
14. Concurrently:
    (a) Make staff separation decisions, with priorities so actual separations will be coordinated with staff needs
    (b) Train those staff members in all departments who will work on or with the new system
    (c) Arrange with Personnel for staged separation interviews with staff members who will no longer be needed, as the old returns dwindle and increasing proportion of returns come in on the new questionnaires
15. Start full operations with the new system

When Sally brought the plan to Steve, he was satisfied and took it to the Operations Manager who, having seen the budget figures, gave approval to proceed. He asked Steve by when he expected to be operational. When Steve told him that he hoped to have completed all the steps in about six months, the Operations Manager asked to be kept informed of progress and offered help should it be needed.

A note to the reader: Please look at the steps that Sally had included in her plan and analyze them critically from the perspective of technical and leadership-in-management issues. You will undoubtedly come to the conclusion that they are heavily weighted in favor of ensuring that the technical considerations are satisfied. Less emphasis is on the non-technical issues.

Back in his office, Steve called Sally to review specifically what decisions had to be made. They were both reading the book on the Eight-Questions Model. Though they had just started, they decided that they would use the concept on the challenges they were facing.

The analysis below, which is being made by observers without intimate knowledge of the environment, is not the same as the thoughts in Sally and

Steve's minds are likely to be. Without knowledge of relevant actions that had been taken in previous situations, it is not possible to determine which of the eight questions may not be relevant. The analysis points to most of the issues that might deserve consideration by Steve and Sally, if there were no previous relevant actions.[1]

ANALYSIS, STEVE AND SALLY'S CHALLENGE—PLANNING FOR MORE EFFICIENT OPERATIONS

The analysis below is based on reasonably extensive knowledge of the 8-Questions model but is not intended to be fully exhaustive or authoritative. There are additional valid thoughts that might occur to others who are well acquainted with the model or use another sound model. The purpose in providing the analysis is to show one reasonably sound approach.

Step 1—Desired Outcome Conditions

In the scenario this step is ignored though it is highly recommended in the literature (Kepner & Tregoe, 1965, 1981); it could include:

- Higher profits
- A reliable scanning process with minimal errors that will meet projected reductions in the cost of entering data from questionnaires
- Efficient operation of all departments affected by the scanning process to ensure lowest overall costs for all activities

---

1. Please note again, as was pointed out in Chapter 3 and the appendix of Chapter 11 that, when identifying the desirable outcome elements, and deciding on goal areas and goals, there are five groups of issues to consider:
   - The technical/functional issues
   - The communications needs of the situation
   - Issues to ensure that the necessary and desirable competencies will be available where needed
   - Issues related to ensuring that stakeholder satisfaction will be as high as possible, but definitely not so low as to create obstacles
   - Issues related to appropriate participation

   As was also mentioned in Chapters 3 and 11, most people, and especially those with experience, can easily identify many of the technical/functional things that should be considered for action. It is the other four, the communications, competence, satisfaction, and participation issues that are often either neglected or ignored. A major benefit of the use of a comprehensive sound model, such as the Eight-Questions Model, is to help decision makers and planners think of these latter issues and give them equal attention so the process will be more comprehensive and thus of higher quality, at least from the leadership perspective.

- Capital outlays within budget
- High level of staff competence in all affected departments, not only for transition tasks, but also for those that are needed for quality monitoring, troubleshooting, and for working with new procedures that may be developed
- High level of staff satisfaction despite the possible reduction in work force
- No impact, or a favorable one, on customers
- Smooth transition from the current system to the more comprehensive scanning process

It should be noted here, as it was in Chapter 3 that communications, competence, satisfaction, and participation, are the primary purely non-technical aspects of the desirable outcome. The others involve technical issues at least as much as non-technical ones. Even relatively unsophisticated managers with less than average leadership competence are likely to identify the first three outcome elements and the last one as desirable. It is attention to communications, competence, satisfaction, and participation that distinguishes the more competent leaders from the others. Competence and satisfaction, as mentioned previously should always be considered when deciding on desirable outcome conditions.

As mentioned previously, in situation analyses with the 8-Questions model, the listed items are only matters that could be considered—not steps that should actually be taken.

Step 2—Assessment of the Eight Questions for Relevance:

Key word: *communications*	relevant
Key word: *participation*	relevant
Key words: *competence, learning, selection*	relevant
Key word: *satisfaction*	relevant
Key words: *progress and performance reviews*	relevant
Key words: *coordination, cooperation, and conflict*	relevant
Key words: *norms, ethics...*	relevant
Key words: *goals and plans*	relevant

Step 3—Review of Relevant Questions

Below is a discussion of many of the issues deserving consideration with respect to the situation in this scenario. They involve thought of many steps that might be relevant. Some of these need not be considered at this time, but recording them for possible future review, and possible action, might be useful.

Question 1—Key Word: Communications

The issues in this question require:

- Ensuring timely communication on everything about progress on each goal/project, by and to all those who work on it and/or are affected by it (up, down and sideways), through channels, when appropriate, or otherwise directly
- Ensuring communication, through channels when appropriate, or directly on all other matters to those who might expect to be informed, with requests for feedback, where appropriate

Considering communications is always important; had Sally and Steve been more familiar with the 8 questions they might have prepared a list of desirable outcome conditions. With or without them, they might have realized that communications with customers need to be considered in the plan.

Question 2—Key Word: Participation

Participation (the extent of participation by the respective participant(s) would be determined by the relevant factors discussed in Chapter 5, such as functional expertise and job role, acceptance sensitivity as needed, work maturity, structure, and 'other factors'. Participation started with the Operations Manager involving the managers reporting to him, in deciding to proceed with investigation of the idea and in setting the outlines of the overall plan (evaluation, budget, approval). Like communications, participation applies in every plan to achieve a desired outcome condition.

The examples from Sally's list, below, show who might do the work and who might be involved in making relevant decisions:

1. Analyze the impact of the program to estimate how many staff members, and which ones, may have to be laid off .
   - Sally, first alone and then review with Steve
2. Jointly with a Personnel staff member designated by the Personnel manager, prepare and issue specific communications about the tentative plans, to the entire staff
   - Steve and/or Sally, first with the Personnel manager and then with the appropriate person from Personnel
3. Speak with each staff member who might be affected, in individual meetings, to explain what might happen and how the company will provide help to hold hardship to a minimum.

   - Sally with Steve to decide what and how to communicate, and then a review with a designated person from Personnel, before speaking with staff members

4. Order one scanner
   - A member of Sally's staff who is familiar with scanners, and Sally to meet with vendor representatives to obtain information on their respective offerings. Later, Sally in meetings with that staff member, possibly Steve, and maybe also someone from Purchasing, designated by the Purchasing manager, who might have useful suggestions for selection of vendor, decision on selection of scanner to be purchased.
5. Finalize the questionnaire, jointly with Marketing and Public Relations
   - One or two members of Sally's staff and a member of the Data Input section, as assigned by Bill. Alternatively, Sally might prepare the draft alone and then review it with these people; a final review by appropriate professionals from Marketing and Public Relations either jointly or separately, and possibly with Steve would finalize the questionnaire
6. Authorize the consultant to proceed with program development
   - Sally, possibly after consulting with staff members who had previous contact with the consultant and with Purchasing, would meet with Purchasing and the consultant, and possibly with Steve to finalize the contract terms
7. Arrange with Public Relations and Marketing to make a pilot mailing, as soon as the questionnaires are ready, and to prepare for a second one soon thereafter
   - Sally and the respective, designated staff members in Public Relations and Marketing
8. Process the returns from the first half of the first pilot mailing without any new equipment, entering the data into the data base by hand, as was done previously with the old questionnaires
   - Decisions for this processing would be made by Sally with Bill who might involve one or more of the staff members from that department

   In addition, to the items on Sally's list, had she added a program for communications with customers, that program would be developed and implemented jointly by the Sales and Marketing departments, possibly with participation by Sally to help ensure technical accuracy.

Please notice that, in this example, participation does not seem to follow the standard pattern of participation at the top first and then at lower organizational levels. That is true, in part, because the entire project proceeds without involvement by the operations manager, other than the initial delegation of the project to Steve—with a minor limitation—to submit the budget and obtain approval before proceeding.

Steve is, in effect, the top manager on the project and Sally, as his deputy, arranges for appropriate participation of people in other departments—always in consultation with the highest person who needs to become involved. That person, then, arranges for participation of staff members by designating individuals.

For the remaining questions (3 through 8) the discussion below merely lists issues that an 8-Questions (or similar) analysis of the scenario *might* raise; some may duplicate issues raised by the desired outcome conditions. As was mentioned previously, such duplication is likely to be beneficial since it provides greater assurance that all issues have been considered. All the issues listed below could be phrased in the form of questions (see the first two items under Question 4)

Question 3—Key Words: Competence, Learning, Selection

- Analysis of training needs for those staff members who will work with the new system (in preparation for goal 14b) (Question: What training needs might exist among those staff who work on(in)...?)
- Development of training programs based on the analysis (Question: What training programs might be beneficial...?)
- Selection and training of trainer(s)
- Training of programmers so they can effectively integrate the consultant's program into the existing system
- Selection and training of programmer(s) who would be competent to effectively remedy any program problems that may develop
- Monitoring of effectiveness of the training
- Ensuring that managers have competence in providing appropriate signs of appreciation for staff member contributions and are highly competent in counseling
- Development of competence to apply the 8-Questions model to decisions at all levels of the organization

Question 4—Key Word: Satisfaction

- Minimizing the negative impact of stress from the content and timing of communications with staff members—those who will be laid off, those who might be laid off, and those whose jobs appear to be safe. (It must be kept in mind that telling someone that his or her job is secure will translate into insecure feelings by anyone who does not get that message. Promises to keep that information confidential are notoriously unreliable.)

- Ensuring that all staff members—those involved in the workforce reduction and all others—are aware that everything reasonably possible is done to help affected staff members minimize the impact on their personal and work lives, including extensive efforts to find positions for displaced staff members
- A review of the other issues discussed in Question 5.3 about effective use of performance evaluations to determine how they can help to achieve the highest possible level of satisfaction of staff members.
- Ensuring that staff members receive appropriate signs of appreciation for not-totally-routine contributions in helping with a smooth transition to the new system
- Consideration of bonuses and other tangible rewards related to significant savings
- Minimizing any negative impact of the transition so it will be as stress-free as possible for staff members who are retained

Question 5—Key words: Progress and Performance Reviews

- Establishment of procedures (if they do not already exist) to ensure that there are regular reviews during which progress on projects and goals (or plans) is reviewed, and additional support that may be needed from the respective manager is explored
- Recommendation to review procedures for performance reviews and performance appraisal (if indicated by lack of adequate performance reviews and/or effective performance evaluations.)

Question 6—Key words: Coordination, Cooperation and Conflict

- With Sally as the primary coordinator with other departments and with appropriate participation and communication, no serious coordination challenges, if any, are likely to arise; however, a review if existing written and commonly practiced procedures may still be desirable
- Consideration of intra- and inter-department cooperation challenges that might arise, monitoring cooperation to notice any arising problems and possible strategies for dealing with them
- If there is no well-established approach on management of conflicts/disputes (including awareness of manager-of-conflict/internal-mediator concept, and related norms), consideration of steps to create such an approach, including those that could ensure appropriate training of managerial staff members, and of all or selected other staff members

Questions 7—Key Words: Norms, Organizational Justice, Ethics, Positive Discipline, Counseling

- Steps to ensure that positive work norms survive the trauma of the reorganization
- Identifying norms related to dealing with conflict and those of individual staff members that may be at odds with desirable organizational norms
- Identifying and implementing steps to bring highest possible level of alignment of organization and staff member norms, including desirable manager training on these issues
- Evaluation of steps that could be taken to measure and enhance the level of positive discipline
- Evaluation of staff views of organizational justice and desirable actions based on the findings
- Review of manager competence for counseling, and developmental programs if indicated

Question 8—Key Words: Goals and Plans

The discussion in this section refers primarily to formal goals, even though there is only a minor mention of goals in the scenario. Still, much of Question 8 is built around formal goals and therefore it is appropriate to speak of them in this analysis. However, it should not be difficult to see how much the same thinking would apply to plans, though they are referred to only in the beginning of the discussion,

On each one of the specific problems, challenges, and opportunities being addressed in this scenario, as well as in every situation, the question should be raised, whether a goal should be set or whether the result should be achieved with plans but without a formal goal (since a team and/or individual can work only on a limited number of goals at one time). Obviously, even without formal goals, there may still be timelines that have to be met.

Once that first question has been answered, at each unit of the organization, it is necessary to ask what formal goals or plans might be appropriate to support the effort to achieve the desired outcomes, and how goals should be expressed (with adequate measurement criteria so the extent of their achievement can be determined—see Chapter 11).

Some of the actions that need to be taken to fully meet the challenges inherent in the situation may not call for goals, but may be either just action steps (see Chapter 11 for the distinction) or be so urgent as to require immediate attention.

In the example scenario, as in any real situation, the issues behind the goals question apply not only to the highest level manager, the Operations

Manager in this case, but to all managers who are involved with projects generated by the challenges. It applies to their own goals as well as to the goals of the staff members that report to them. Most goals are set with, and for, staff members who will work on a goal in support of the departmental or team goal, with appropriate participation, of course.

The situation in the scenario is not an emergency and the problem, while deserving immediate attention, does allow for the setting of goals. The goals and tasks that become apparent at the outset of the planning process, those that flow directly from the desired outcome conditions, could be considered as temporary. Then, after some participation, and brief thought to the other questions, they would probably be augmented with additional goals and tasks later on. Some of them are not for managers or staff members in the MIS department. These may require consultation and coordination with the respective other department, or possibly even with the Operations Manager. In the scenario immediately apparent goals and actions that might be appropriate for the respective teams, and/or for individuals, could be on all the items in Sally's plan.

Since that plan is very thorough, there are few additional specific results on which goals or actions might be considered. However, the following possible goal areas might be worth thinking about—they were triggered by the desired outcome conditions and a quick scan of the eight questions:

1. Consideration of the competence question, brought by thought of the desired outcome on 'High level of staff competence…' might highlight the need for development of in-house competence to deal with scanner program problems as might occur
2. The scan might also suggest other competence development, by identifying learning needs and management of learning programs to satisfy them. This might involve goals for those whose work is indirectly involved in the scanning changes, such as customer list updates and related tasks, and others who may be involved only peripherally, such as the marketing people.
3. The 'High level of staff morale…' outcome might bring thought of goals on
   - Obtaining cooperation from Human Resources to find as many job opportunities as possible for staff members who will be affected by a staff reduction
   - Coordinating with Human Resources to assist with timing of possible internal placements of staff members
   - Other steps to reduce dissatisfaction by staff members that are likely to result from staff reduction, and related changes in work-

load and assignments might bring goals so the highest possible level of work satisfaction can be achieved and maintained.
   - Goals for steps to anticipate and effectively deal with the heightened stress that has to be anticipated as a result of the expected changes in staffing and work routines
   - Goals on the specifics of any bonuses that might be given if the anticipated savings materialize
4. A goal to evaluate Sally's competence in providing signs of appreciation for staff members, and for enhancing her actual implementation

In addition:

- Consideration of coordination might bring
  - Thought of a goal for preparation of a written procedures manual for the scanning, including basic troubleshooting
  - Thought of goals for data quality monitoring procedures to ensure high quality of data entry of returns accepted by the scanners and of those that are rejected by them
- Consideration of progress reviews might bring thought of preparation of goals for productivity monitoring procedures

As was pointed out above, this is not an exhaustive list, but shows the process for deciding the types of goal areas that deserve consideration either in conjunction with other steps to achieve the stated outcome conditions, or at a later date. Still this list of additional matters that might be worthwhile to consider in the plan, shows how the eight considerations can be helpful to identify those that might otherwise be overlooked.

As was also pointed out previously, it is desirable to determine which of the things that have to be accomplished deserve formal goals, and who is to have primary responsibility to accomplish each one.

This is where the importance/urgency criteria should be considered as well as the limit on the number of goals for each person or team, and the need for coordination with other departments.

Examples of formal goals that might be used for items on Sally's list, in appropriate language to allow measurement, is given below. The other listed accomplishments in Sally's plan might be worked on without formal goals since most are tied to those with goals. Still, as much as possible, they would have informally planned steps/timelines to achieve them. The nonsequential numbers and letters in this list correspond to those in Sally's plan. Actual goals that might be set would depend on the number of goals on which the respective person who would have primary responsibility, can work simultaneously. It would, of course, be possible to initiate formal goals on some of the other expected results after some earlier ones have been reached. Each goal/action step drafted below is for the person with primary responsibility to achieve the respective one and should be arrived at with appropriate participation between that staff member and the manager. Please note that each one is sufficiently specific so it is possible to determine how well it has been achieved with the resources that are either implied or stated. In addition to the ones on the list below would be the goals for the goal areas added by the scan of the eight questions.

2. By (date) prepare, jointly with Personnel, specific communications about the tentative plans, and issue them, after review by the Operations Manager, to all affected staff members and those who would want to know them
5. Jointly with Marketing and Public Relations, test the questionnaire with at least 100 customers, and finalize it by (date)
7. Arrange with Public Relations and Marketing to make a pilot mailing by (date), or as soon as the questionnaires are ready, if earlier, and prepare to mail a second one (number of weeks) later
11. Use the scanner on the returns from the second pilot mailing and make any final adjustments to the questionnaire that may be necessary by (date) (this is an example of a goal which could be initiated after the first pilot is completed).
12. By (date) arrange with Public Relations and Marketing to proceed with the new questionnaires after they have been pilot tested and revised if necessary, on all future mailings (this is another example of a goal that could be initiated at a later time after some other goals have been reached).

14b. By (date) complete training of staff members who will work on or with the new system and confirm full competence based on criteria to be established in advance (please note the quality specified by the goal; this goal could also be initiated at a later time after some other goals have been reached)

15. By (date) start full operations with the new system.

    (a) Prepare, and pilot test a written manual for the scanning, including basic troubleshooting, by (date)
    (b) By (date) complete data quality monitoring procedures, arrange for review by (departments) and initiate their use (weeks) after the first pilot
    (c) By (date) have at least two staff members competent to deal with scanner program problems as might develop and confirm their competence with simulated difficult potential problems
    (d) By (date) establish guidelines for any bonuses that might be given if the anticipated savings materialize and obtain approval from the General Manager

It is worthwhile to note here that, even with a careful planner such as Sally, using the Eight-Questions Model can make plans more thorough and include relevant items—especially those pertaining to communications, competence, satisfaction and norms, that might otherwise be overlooked.

Please note that issues that were not adequately considered in the scenario, prior to this analysis, lie primarily in the non-functional issues such as those pertaining to communications, participation, goals, satisfaction, competence, etc.

It might also be worthwhile to repeat a paragraph from Chapter 3: At this point it may seem as though this analysis process is far too cumbersome to conduct with all, and even with the important decisions and plans. As has already been pointed out, that is not the case, however, for three reasons: a) once the habit to ask the questions and to evaluate relevance has been established, the thought process occurs with great speed (as speed-chess masters, pianists, and even typing has demonstrated); b) in a real situation, as distinct from a hypothetical one, there is a history which indicates that several, and possibly most of the issues that the questions raise have been resolved in prior decisions or plans and need not be addressed again—possibly making only a few questions relevant; c) in some instances, since fewer matters will be overlooked, errors can be avoided, thus eliminating the need for corrective steps that could possibly take considerable time; d) most important, though, even in urgent cases, a quick run through of all eight main questions might bring highly beneficial results. That is especially true since the structure provided by the eight questions may often bring faster analysis of the situation than a careful traditional one.

CHAPTER 14

MANAGEMENT, LEADERSHIP, MOTIVATION THEORIES, AND RESEARCH ABOUT THE ROLE OF DECISIONS IN MANAGEMENT PERFORMANCE

MANAGEMENT THEORY AND CONCEPTS: ORIGINS AND PATHWAYS

The problem is to organize
This monumental enterprise
So that, to see that all are boarded,
Both need, and reality are rewarded.

—Adapted from Kenneth Boulding,
Principles of Economic Policy, 10

Introduction

While most of this book discusses matters important *for practicing* leadership, this chapter discusses what is considered to be leadership. In very brief sketches, it traces the evolution of theories relevant to management

Planning, Common Sense, and Superior Performance, pages 153–176

and leadership and thus provides a foundation for the concepts discussed in this book. These theories either describe what is or what should be and provide preciously little guidance for what a leader or manager can/should do to make them a reality.

Research and theories on management started to emerge toward the end of the industrial revolution, as many organizations and businesses grew to considerable size. Frederick Taylor, an American engineer, who is often seen as the father of what was called either 'Management Science', or 'Scientific Management', and others, began to study worker productivity (Taylor, 1911). The objective was to find optimal ways to design the jobs of production workers and to determine how those workers might best be selected, trained, paid, and supervised. The effort led to standard costing, method study, time-and-motion study, worker performance standards, and other measurement techniques. In an indirect way, Taylor is also the father of Total Quality Management (TQM) concepts because they evolved from 'Value Engineering', a scientific management technique that derived from the management science ideas and was popular during the 1950s.

Soon, question arose about the ways in which managers and supervisors contributed to productivity. Here, Henry Fayol, a French mining engineer, led the way (Fayol, 1916/1949).

The Fayol Cycle and the Eight-Questions Model

For more than 90 years after its original publication in French, Fayol's view of managerial work as a cycle (Fayol, 1916/1949) is still a major foundation for management education. It continues to be taught as a fundamental concept in most basic management courses.

Fayol depicted the manager's function as a circle of planning (defining ends and means); organizing (providing for the necessary equipment, resources, and people); commanding (supervising subordinates); coordinating (ensuring that equipment, resources and people are effectively interacting); controlling (ensuring that outcomes are consistent with plans); and back to planning. The inclusion of 'commanding' sounds strange to us today, but in the early part of the 20th century, it was expected that a manager issued orders, commanded. In a similar vein, today we do not speak of 'subordinates' as was the practice well into the 1950s, but refer to people, who report to a manager, as staff members or associates.

Most modern management books continue to be organized around versions of Fayol's cycle. However, while planning and organizing have usually remained, some of the other terms have been replaced by the various writers with words like executing, implementing, staffing, leading and follow-up. In a way these words reflect more current views of the functions of managers.

Two major textbooks (Robbins, 1991; Plunkett & Attner, 1992) use two different lists: planning/organizing/leading/controlling and planning/organizing/staffing/directing/controlling, respectively. Other books have used words such as coordinating, implementing, and evaluating, as part of the series.

Fayol's cycle provides a general guide to managerial work, regardless of the manager's functional or organizational environment. However, as a basic foundation for management thinking and decision making, it has a number of shortcomings.

Deficiencies of the Fayol Cycle

As a practical, useful model that can help managers at all levels, in all types of public and private organizations, the Fayol cycle has several significant drawbacks:

1. It is fuzzy with respect to two major responsibilities of managers: a) ensuring appropriate competence, and b) developing and/or maintaining a satisfying climate.
2. It does not provide useful criteria for the evaluation of a manager's performance as leader, as distinct from performance in the functional specialties such as operations, marketing, finance, or entrepreneur, or the type of organizations such as manufacturing or service business, government agency, health care, education, etc.
3. It fails to provide sufficiently clear and practical guidelines for decisions, and for plans, that managers can use to evaluate them objectively, as a foundation for improvements prior to implementation, and for corrective steps when there are deviations from expected results.

It might be possible to create an expanded version of Fayol's cycle that can overcome the shortcomings. However, the idea of a cycle fails to provide a descriptive and prescriptive image of a manager's multi-faceted, interlocking and overlapping activities. A different model could be far more useful, especially if it starts from a universally accepted concept. That concept could be that decisions are the foundation of all managerial actions and that they therefore should consider all the responsibilities of a manager, possibly as discussed in this book.

Comparing the Eight-Questions Model with the Fayol Cycle

It might be useful here to compare the Fayol cycle with the eight questions in this book, since they cover the same ground from different perspectives.

Some conceptual testing needs to be done, to see whether the eight questions, and the issues behind them can indeed fully replace the items in Fayol's cycle, however they may be defined. If they satisfy this requirement it will then be necessary to see whether they can serve the purpose of decision and plan guidelines better than the concepts in Fayol's cycle.

With respect to *planning*, it would seem that managers are effective in planning if they consider, at least:

- Practicing appropriate participation (including delegation),in decision-making and planning
- Effectively communicating about the plans with stakeholders, individually and in groups,
- Seeing to it that challenging and realistic goals are set (including those on direction and vision) and specific plans are prepared on how to achieve them,
- Ensuring that the distinction between goals and actions steps is reflected in accountability of managers, staff members and teams, and
- Ensuring coordination and cooperation.

These are all items from the eight questions in the model.

The same approach can be used to see whether the issues in the 8-Questions Model satisfy the need for *organizing*. It would seem that managers will ensure that the organization is organized to achieve its plans as well as that can be done, by, at least:

- Practicing appropriate participation in decision-making and planning (including delegation),
- Effectively communicating about the plans with stakeholders, individually and in groups,
- Ensuring that the distinction between goals and actions steps is reflected in accountability of staff members and teams,
- Ensuring coordination with appropriate procedures, and stimulating cooperation,
- Ensuring that potentially damaging conflicts/disputes are competently anticipated, prevented where possible, and managed,
- Ensuring that appropriate norms exist and are respected
- Fostering a climate of positive discipline
- Ensuring selection of highly qualified candidates for all vacant positions, from within and from outside

- Leading toward determination of what competence improvement is needed, what will be useful, and how to bring high competence levels efficiently
- Leading toward most effective use of competence strengths of staff members and/or teams, and
- Ensuring that performance evaluation brings a more motivational climate

Space does not permit here to provide similar proof for each one of the other terms that have been used as part of the Fayol cycle. However it should be fairly obvious, that consideration of the eight questions would show that all the terms used to describe the Fayol cycle, including leading, controlling, staffing, directing, coordinating, implementing, and evaluating, are covered with equal thoroughness as planning and organizing.

Fayol also defined a number of "Principles of Management" including division of labor and unity of command (the principle that one person should report to only one manager or supervisor). These concepts, too, have been modified, or partially replaced.

A Different Direction for Theories

A different direction for management theories came by accident, from a famous attempt to determine how working conditions (the satisfaction of employees) affected productivity. At Western Electric Company's Hawthorne plant in Chicago, during the late 1920s, among other experiments, six young women were detached from a department with hundreds of assemblers. In their separated room they were under close observation and given friendly attention. Their work environment was altered, first favorably with longer breaks and other changes such as better lighting, and then made less and less desirable. At one point, rest periods were eliminated entirely. Through it all, work output increased.

During the extensive Hawthorne experiments, the various aspects of human behavior in the work environment were studied in depth for the first time. Topics included group formation and development (formally and informally), behavioral influences on productivity, communications, and the sources of morale.

As interpreted by Elton Mayo (1933), these studies heralded the beginning of the human relations theory of management, often referred to as the behavioral sciences in management.

Today there are two primary branches of this body of theory: leadership, and motivation.

The impact of motivation and leadership theories on management education and development reached a peak during the 1950s and 1960s when the most significant, broad gauged research was performed. Since then, the efforts of scholars and other researchers has concentrated on correcting or adjusting for inadequacies in the original theories, and to introduce other ideas, some of which are highly subjective and even controversial. In effect, what has happened since then, is a fractionalization of behavioral theories, with overlaps and internal contradictions. Only sporadically have there been significant attempt to create bridges between these theories, and practical application and use. Total Quality Management is one of the most successful attempts of such a bridge.

Unfortunately, this field of studies continues to offer more questions than answers, and is full of competing and conflicting models and theories. As Moorhead and Griffin (1992, page xix) have phrased it so aptly:

> The field of organizational behavior, still in its infancy as a science, remains full of competing and conflicting models and theories. There are few laws or absolute principles that dictate proper conduct for organizational members or predict with certainty their behaviors. The role of human resources in the long-term viability of any business or not-for-profit enterprise is nevertheless recognized as enormously significant. Other resources—financial, informational, and material—are also essential, but only human resources are virtually boundless in their potential impact (positive or negative) on the organization.

Leadership theories, in particular, are having a hard time. In *Handbook of Leadership: A Survey of Theory and Research*, (Stogdill, 1974) noted that there are as many definitions of leadership as there are persons who have attempted to define the concept. In *Leadership: Strategies for Taking Charge*, Bennis and Nanus (1985) referred to leadership as the most studied and least understood topic of any in the social sciences. Colleges and universities offer a plethora of courses and workshops on the topic of leadership, undaunted by the challenge of teaching that which cannot be defined and is not yet well understood. Unfortunately, managers who participate in such courses, often emerge with a frustrating sense that leadership is akin to the Abominable Snowman whose footprints are everywhere but who is nowhere to be seen.

The question of whether or not a discipline of management had developed[1] continues to occupy the concern of both academics and practitio-

---

1. While the discipline of 'management' may be subject to question, there is no doubt that there are disciplines within the concept of management that are well developed. This applies to Operations Research, Finance, Marketing, Human Resources, Information Systems, etc. It is the human relations aspect of Management, and Leadership, that are the focus of criticisms.

ners. Surely, if such a discipline exists, a common definition of management and leadership, together with a body of consistent literature should be available. This, unfortunately, is not the case. Many have argued for understanding management as a general concept rooted in organizational theory, as understanding human behavior in organizations, as problem-solving, as decision-making, and as a social process. None of these approaches can stand alone. The distinguished management scholar, Harold Koontz (1980), after a lifetime of study, lamented the existence of a continuing "Management Theory Jungle" composed of these schools of thought: Empirical (case study); Interpersonal Behavior; Group Behavior; Cooperative Social System; Sociotechnical Systems; Decision Theory; Systems; Mathematical (management science); Contingency (situational); Managerial Roles; Operational (management function). Koontz even commented that the situation had actually deteriorated in the 20 years since his earlier review of the state of the art.

Part of the reason for lack of progress may be that there is not much, of a comprehensive nature, that new research is likely to uncover. Then, there might be the pressure of more rewarding ideas to concentrate on. During the 1980s and 1990s, in addition to continuing growth of computer-related concepts, attention shifted to issues that would help businesses overcome the increasingly fierce domestic and foreign competitive pressures, and assist government agencies to cope with the ever more severe budget cuts. These issues addressed organizational culture and organizational strategies that led to Total Quality Management and quality circles, productivity that led to reengineering, restructuring, and mergers, and most recently, to interest in organizational learning.

Conclusion

This is the situation today. The many and frequently bewildering theories often confuse more than clarify and do not provide practical guidelines for decisions and action, especially those that concern the leadership aspects of management. The search for such answers continues to lead us to seek solace in those who promise easy answers to complex realities. So we tried focusing on topics such as Time Management (Lakein, 1973), One-minute Management (Blanchard and Johnson, 1982), Habits of Effective People (Covey, 1989), in Search of, and Passion for, Excellence (Peters & Waterman, 1982; Peters & Austin, 1985), and transformational leadership. While none of these are irrelevant, they seem to have their day, deliver less than they promise, and lead us to start the search for deeper knowledge all over again.

All, however, bring useful insights that can help in some situations—but they fail to concentrate on the practical application of what we have learned from the theories, by providing answers to two questions: What does management/leadership mean to me? How can I best manage and lead in a given situation? To answer these questions you need something that is important at every managerial level—a comprehensive approach that fits all decisions/plans, and that enhance managerial competence as well as leadership competence. To some extent, such an approach can be found in the use a series of comprehensive questions with every decision and plan, such as the 8-Questions Model. Figure 14.1, *Leadership Theories and Their Practical Applications*, at the end of discussion of theories, depicts how all theories converge to provide a foundation for each one of the 8 questions in the Model—the practical applications of the theories.

LEADERSHIP THEORIES

Introduction

The following will be briefly discussed in this chapter:

- Trait Theory
- Behavioral Theories
- Contingency Theories
- Other Theories

The theories discussed here are not meant to be comprehensive—they represent a listing of only the ideas that have had major impact on the thinking of others. When appropriate, one or very few names are associated here with each theory or group of theories. In most cases, others have contributed to the respective theories, as we know them today. However, the researchers or thinkers who are listed have either originated the concept, have provided a thorough overview, or are most often considered to have made the most important contributions.

Leadership is widely seen as the ability to influence the behavior of others (usually toward the achievement of some end result). In this regard, power and authority are, of course, important elements of leadership. However, these external influences aside, theories discussed here address primarily the personal characteristics, and behaviors, and even perception of followers, which are believed to make some leaders more successful than others. The complexities of the issues involved, led to a very large number of theories. Brief highlights are given below.

Trait Theory

Trait theory (Ghiselli, 1963; Stogdill, 1974) emphasizes the importance of personal characteristics and traits of leaders in shaping the quality of their leadership. These traits include physical, mental, and cultural attributes, including charisma, decisiveness, intelligence, self-confidence and energy, which make some leaders more successful than others.

Behavioral Theories

Behavioral theories address the question whether there is some identifying behavior of leaders that can make them more effective. There are a number of such theories. The two-dimensional theories (task vs. relationship), discussed below, are the most widely known:

a. Initiate Structure

One theory (based on studies at Ohio State University; Fleishman, Harris & Burtt, 1955), states that leaders "initiate structure" such as assigning group members to tasks, and that they expect that standards are met. They also show "consideration" for their staff members, such as respect for their ideas, concern for developing trust, and interest in their work satisfaction. The most effective leader, according to this theory, usually is one who can balance these aspects of leadership, though there are some problems that such a leader faces.

b. Employee Orientation and Production Orientation

Other behavioral theories, based on studies at University of Michigan (Likert, 1961; Kahn & Katz, 1960) use two dimensions, "employee orientation" and "production orientation", as measures of leader effectiveness. These studies found that groups with leaders who have high employee orientation, perform best.

c. Concern for People and Concern for Production

A third type of behavioral theories, based on the Managerial (or Leadership) Grid Model (Blake & Mouton, 1964, 1968) are similar to those discussed in b. above. These theories group the behaviors of managers/leaders into "concern for people" and "concern for production". According to studies by two researchers, Blake and Mouton, the leaders whose style combine high concern for both dimensions, led the most productive teams.

Contingency Theories

There are many contingency theories that attempt to look at leadership characteristics and skills from the perspective of the needs of the situation in which the leader has to act. The most widely known of these are the Autocratic-Democratic Continuum Model, Leadership-Participation Theory, the Hersey-Blanchard Situational Model, Fiedler's Contingency Theory, and the Path-Goal Theory.

a. Tannenbaum and Schmidt Autocratic-Democratic Continuum Model

The Tannenbaum and Schmidt Autocratic-Democratic Continuum Model (Tannenbaum and Schmidt, 1958/73) holds that a leader can, and should choose from among an infinite number of possible combinations of authority by the manager, and authority granted to followers (staff members) when making a decision. The model depicts these combinations ranging from complete control by the manager over decisions, to the other extreme where the members of the staff have wide freedom in determining what should be done. According to this model, the most effective leaders are those who have the best batting average in choosing the most appropriate mix between 'Boss-centered' leadership, and 'Subordinate-centered' leadership (the terms actually used originally by the authors in 1958) for any specific decision. The model does not speak of involvement by other stakeholders, though it also does not specifically exclude them.

b. Leadership-Participation Theory

Leadership-Participation Theory (Vroom & Yetton, 1973), though focused primarily on decision making, is a refinement of the Autocratic-Democratic Continuum Model. It selects five points from the many possible ones along the continuum. A leader should choose the measure of control on the basis of the answers to several questions which concern the extent to which the leader has the needed information, how acceptable a specific possible solution would be to the staff, the likelihood of conflicts/disputes, etc.

Both a. and b. above are discussed in Question 2.2, (*how,* and on *what* part of the decision or plan should the participants be involved)

c. The Hersey-Blanchard Situational Leadership Model

The Hersey-Blanchard Situational Leadership Model (1969 and 1982), is based on the authors' original work on 'Life-Cycle' need of staff members, for appropriate leadership. It concludes that there is need for maximum help and guidance for the least mature level of staff members or teams, where experience, achievement motivation, and willingness and ability to accept responsibility, are at their lowest. Greatest freedom is appropriate at the highest maturity level.

d. Fiedler's Contingency Theory

Fiedler's Contingency Theory, (Fiedler, 1967) which is more comprehensive, states that leader effectiveness is determined by the leader's style, and by the impact of the situation on the decision. Leaders should identify situations (based on position power, leader-member relations, and task structure) where they are effective and those where they perform less well, and learn to better align situations and personal style.

e. Path-Goal Theory

Path-Goal Theory (House, 1971), like other contingency theories, is based on the relationship between leader behavior and the elements of the situation. Path-Goal theory concentrates on the type of assistance to staff members, which a leader should provide in various situations and environments, to help them achieve their goals and greater work satisfaction.

Other Theories

a. Leader–Member Relations Theory (LMX)

Leader–Member Relations (Exchange) (Graen, & Cashman, 1975). Theory contributes the importance of direct, one-on-one relationships between the leader and individual staff members. In most organizational units, leaders have a tendency to establish more favorable work relations with some members of the group. . This creates 'in' groups and leads to different levels of performance, work satisfaction, and turnover, based on whether staff members perceive themselves to be in the in-group or not.

b. Attribution Theory

Attribution Theory (McElroy, 1982; Martinko, 1995) looks at leadership from a different perspective. It places emphasis on the views of the followers. The characteristics and behaviors that followers consider as appropriate for a good leader, are those that are needed in the respective situation.

c. Charismatic Leadership Theory

Charismatic leadership theory (Conger & Kanungo. 1987) sprung from attribution theory and suggests that followers make attributions of heroic or extraordinary leadership abilities when they observe certain behaviors. Charismatic leaders display admired characteristics including self-confidence, vision, ability to articulate the vision, strong convictions about the vision, behavior that is out of the ordinary, and environmental sensitivity.

d. Transformational Leadership Theory

Transformational Leadership Theory (Burns, 1978; Bennis & Nanus, 1985) also takes a different tack from the other theories, most of which are considered 'transactional' by the proponents of this theory. Transformational leaders are believed to have sufficient influence on followers, that they 'transform' them to subordinate their self-interest to the needs of the organization. In general, transformational leaders are inspirational, intellectually stimulating, and considerate to the individual. Please note that some transformational leaders bring a vision that transforms the organization and gives it new or revised, more successful direction. However, such a vision is not essential. A leader who considers the eight-questions discussed in this book will, undoubtedly achieve the transformation of followers referred to above.

e. Full Range Leadership

Full Range Leadership, (Avolio & Bass, 1995) asserts that leaders who can practice the prescriptions of behavioral and contingency leadership theories, and can be transformational at the same time, are the most effective leaders.

Conclusions from the Leadership Theories

In practical terms, all these theories point in the same direction—competent leaders display behaviors that allow them to have personal influence on followers, beyond the influence that the authority of their positions give them.

Some of these behaviors are due to personal characteristics and traits that inspire confidence—physical appearance, and other attributes of a commanding presence, an engaging personality, possibly something akin to the ability to see and articulate a vision or at least direction, etc. These are all matters that we cannot change or that take a lot of effort and a long time to change. Most of the behaviors, however, are based on the competence to develop a climate in which followers can gain trust and confidence in the leader and in the direction in which he or she is leading the organization. This latter competence is a bundle of skills that can be learned fairly easily and that can effectively link the organization's characteristics and needs to those of its stakeholders.

Matter to consider for decisions and plans and guidelines drawn from a comprehensive, sound, universally applicable and actionable model of questions to ask, can provide a practical approach to applying the lessons that the theories convey. The questions can serve as foundation for learning and honing the skills that can make a manager as inspiring a leader as his or her traits permit. The skills for creating and sustaining a motivational climate are essentially the same as those that achieve high quality leadership. The decision considerations discussed in this book in the form of the 8-Questions Model, or in its predecessors, the 3Cs concept and the Linking Elements (Rausch 1978/85; Rausch & Washbush, 1998), appear to be the best currently available models of practical approaches for to developing these skills.

It is important to note here that these models of management/leadership incorporate the critical elements of both leadership and motivation theories. The issues that the questions ask are central to the leadership and motivation research findings that are discussed from various perspectives in the theories. That is the reason why greater knowledge of the conceptual/theoretical foundations for the questions can make them more useful.

Two points should be kept in mind when thinking of leadership, that have begun to permeate discussion of leadership in more recent years. They are (1) that leadership is often demonstrated by individuals without position authority when they lead in a meeting or elsewhere toward acceptance of an idea, and in their private lives, and (2) that characteristics of followers affect effectiveness of leader attributes and behaviors.

MOTIVATION THEORIES

It has been said, wisely, that we don't want someone to motivate us, but we want a motivational climate where we can find enjoyment and growth in our work.

Introduction

The following will be briefly discussed in this chapter:

- Hierarchy of Needs (Maslow, 1954)
- Theory X and Theory Y (McGregor, 1960)
- Motivation-Hygiene (Herzberg, 1959 and 1968)
- Other Theories

As with the leadership theories, the list below is not meant to be an exhaustive one—just those theories which have had major impact on the thinking of others. Only one name is associated here with each theory. In most cases, others have contributed to the respective theory, as we know it today. However, the name is that of the person who either originated the concept, or is most often considered to have made the most important contribution.

As was pointed out previously, there is much overlap between leadership and motivation theories. This is, of course, understandable since follower motivation is a primary, if not the overarching objective of leadership.

Hierarchy of Needs (Maslow, 1954)

The most widely known work was done by Abraham Maslow, who depicted human needs in a five level pyramid, with basic physiological needs (survival needs such as food and shelter) at the base, safety and security (protection of the survival needs for the future) at the next level, belonging and social activity at the third level, esteem and status at the fourth, and self-realization and fulfillment at the peak. Maslow's statement that satisfaction of lower level needs is a prerequisite for motivation by higher level need, has been widely criticized and much empirical evidence has shown serious flaws in that statement. Dividing those of the levels that can be so divided into what requires financial resources and what can be provided by a manager without expenditures provides foundation for satisfying experiences for staff members (see Question 4.3—What other issues deserve consideration and Rausch, 1978/85, pp. 157–159)

Theory X and Theory Y (McGregor, 1960)

McGregor's scheme of two management assumptions is almost as widely known as Maslow's hierarchy. It has less operational impact because it merely describes two managerial styles:

- Theory X which is based on the assumption that managers have to exercise tight control over every aspect of the productive process because 'workers' are naturally inclined to work as little as possible, to shirk responsibility, etc.
- Theory Y which holds that people do not have an inherent dislike of work and that management's role is to arrange organizational conditions and methods of operation so that people can achieve their own goals best by devoting effort toward organizational objectives.

There is evidence that, by and large, organizations that display a Theory Y style, are more productive and have more positively motivated staffs.

Motivation-Hygiene (Herzberg, 1959, 1968)

At about the same time as McGregor's work, Frederick Herzberg and his group from Case Western University, surveyed professional employees and came to the conclusion that there were factors in the work environment which did not motivate people but which, when absent, had a detrimental effect. He called them 'dissatisfaction avoiders', or hygiene factors. They included salary, fringe benefits, even working conditions such as breaks. On the other hand, the survey showed that the nature of the work itself—achievement, responsibility, recognition and advancement—were the factors which motivated people. "Job Enrichment" programs in which jobs were restructured to bring more intrinsic rewards, which were popular during the 70s, were the result of this work.

Other Theories

Taking off from Maslow, McGregor, and Herzberg, were many other theories, some of which were quite popular for a number of years. They include:

- Three Needs Theory which emphasized achievement, power and affiliation as the key influences on motivation (McClelland, 1961)
- Expectancy Theory (Vroom, 1964) in which the level of motivation is determined by the expectation of the employee that he or she will be able to successfully complete the task, combined with the expectation of the psychological and/or tangible benefits that such success will bring.
- Equity Theory (Adams, 1965) is based on the fact that almost everyone wants to be treated fairly, especially in relation to others. Motivation, lack of it, or de-motivation results from this comparison.
- ERG (Existence, Relatedness and Growth) (Alderfer, 1969) is a modification of the Maslow hierarchy. In a rough sense, 'existence' is equivalent to Maslow's physiological and safety/security needs, 'relatedness' is similar to social and esteem needs and there is great similarity between 'growth' and self-realization.
- Another modification of Maslow's hierarchy is described by Rausch (1978/1985). It separates all but the top (self realization and fulfillment) and bottom (basic physiological) needs into two components—those that can best be satisfied with psychological rewards, and those that require tangible rewards. For instance, there are esteem needs that the manager can satisfy in various ways without spending money, and there are others that, for some people, can only be satisfied with things that cost money.
- Cognitive Evaluation Theory (Deci, 1975) suggests that there are close links between psychological rewards of the work itself (intrinsic moti-

vators) and tangible rewards (extrinsic motivators), with significant implications on compensation strategies.

- Reinforcement Theory (Steers & Porter, 1979; Skinner, 1968) is based on widely researched psychological theories that confirm the ability of recognition or other psychological rewards (positive reinforcement), to encourage repetition of desirable behavior.
- Goal Setting Theory (Locke & Latham, 1984, 1990) suggests that setting 'goals' for, or with, staff members, has strong motivational impact.

There are other motivation theories that are less widely discussed in the literature. Furthermore, there is considerable overlap with leadership theories since it is obvious that effective leadership has a strong motivational component in encouraging followers to support the leader's goals.

It is important to note here, as was also stated earlier in this Chapter, that the 8 questions to ask when making decisions and developing plans, which are introduced in this book, incorporate the critical elements of both leadership and motivation theories. The issues that the questions raise are central to the leadership and motivation findings that are discussed from various perspectives in the theories. That is the reason why greater knowledge of the conceptual/theoretical foundations can make the use of the questions more beneficial. (See Figure 14.1 *Leadership Theories and Their Practical Applications* at the end of this discussion of theories.)

Conclusions from the Motivation Theories

The conclusions from the motivation theories are quite similar to those of the leadership theories. Leadership behaviors that motivate followers inspire them to trust their leader and to have confidence in his or her ability to provide all the components of a satisfying work-life. These are skills that stretch from identifying successful direction, to developing a satisfying climate, to ensuring that followers have confidence in their respective abilities to contribute effectively to the total effort. Usually, though not always, they require significant competence in the interpersonal communications and related skills. Attractive appearance and charismatic personal behaviors, are of course helpful, though not essential.

The skills for creating and sustaining a motivational climate are essentially the same as those that achieve high quality leadership. The 8-Questions Model discussed here as well as its predecessor, the 3Cs concept, also named the Linking Elements concept (Rausch 1978/85, and Rausch and Washbush 1998) appear to be the best currently available models of practical approaches for to developing these skills.

Connecting All Theories with the 8-Questions Model

Figure 14.1 shows how all leadership, motivation, decision-making theories, as well as other theories pertaining to skills such as communications and conflict resolutions can be thought of as converging so they are all accessible to the manager/leader who would like to draw on them for thoughts to apply with respect to the issues in the 8-Questions model. At the same time, the diagram dramatizes the fact that the issues covered by the eight questions satisfy any of the theories that the user would like to apply.

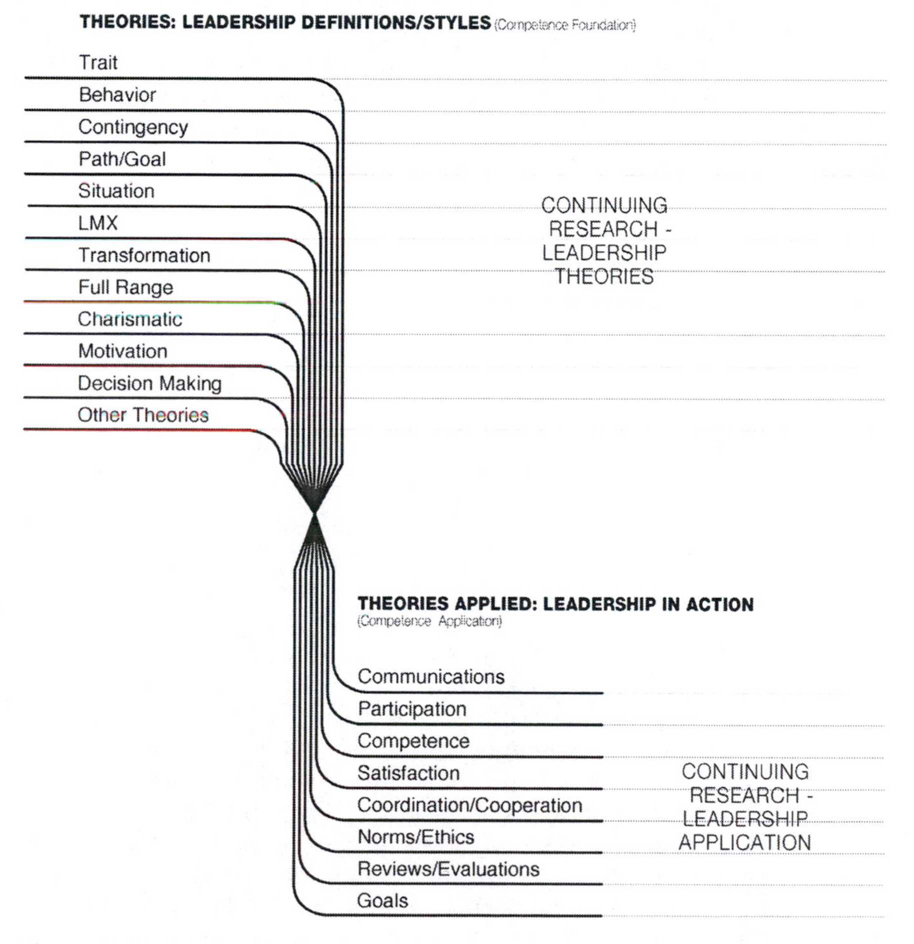

Figure 14.1. Leadership theories and their practical application. © Erwin Rausch.

RESEARCH ABOUT THE ROLE OF DECISIONS AND PLANNING IN MANAGEMENT PERFORMANCE

To set the stage for the detailed discussion of the model described in this book (the eight questions) it is useful to take a look at other thinking about effectiveness in management/leadership and organizations.

Research to Determine What Constitutes Effective Management

Academics, management scientists and human resource managers have tried, in many ways, to define what makes an effective manager. Almost all these attempts have concentrated on identifying skills. This is even true of the very first attempt, by Henry Fayol (Fayol, 1916/1949). Whetten and Cameron (1993) phrased the question in these terms "What constitutes effective management?" In search for an answer, they interviewed 402 highly effective managers in the private and public sectors. They reported on the ten skills most frequently cited by these managers:

1. Verbal communication
2. Managing time and stress
3. Managing individual decisions
4. Recognizing, defining, and solving problems
5. Motivating and influencing others
6. Delegating
7. Setting goals and articulating a vision
8. Self-awareness
9. Team building
10. Managing conflict

It is interesting to note that quality of decisions and plans appear to be buried in the third, fourth, and seventh, of these 10 skills, and that the critically important responsibility of using appropriate participation in decision making and planning is not mentioned at all, though it is undoubtedly hidden in Motivating and influencing others. Equally interesting is the observation that the 10 pertain primarily to issues that were once part of what was then called the behavioral sciences in management. Today it would probably be more appropriate to lump most of them under leadership-in-management skills, as distinct from the technical managerial skills such as marketing, operations, finance, MIS, etc. As pointed out before, the clumsy term "leadership-in-management" is used to differentiate these leadership skills from the much different set of skills, and traits, which distinguish leaders in other fields, such as in the arts, the sciences, social action, charitable causes, most sports, and even in politics to some extent.

Whetten and Cameron compared their conclusions with seven different surveys covering several thousand managers and found considerable conceptual similarity, and agreement, at least with respect to the conclusion—that skills are key to effective management. Two years later, in their comprehensive book on development of management skills (Whetten & Cameron, 1995), they described a management education/development program with a similar, but slightly different list of skills.

It is also useful to note that, of the skills listed, some are more or less fairly distinct, such as verbal communications, managing time and stress, delegating, setting goals (though not "articulating a vision"), and self-awareness. However, managing individual decisions, recognizing, defining and solving problems, and most importantly, motivating and influencing others, are highly complex sets of skills that involve a large number of considerations. In fact, the last one, motivating and influencing, in effect includes all the others, and it is at the core of competent leadership and management. It covers all the leadership issues discussed in this book that, together with technical considerations, can serve as foundation for developing and measuring managerial competence.

Unfortunately, opinions about skills of effective managers, as reported in the different studies cited by Whetten and Cameron (1995), are not a practical basis for measuring quality of management and for developing more competent leaders. Managers know little about what they do not know, and when they are asked about skills of effective managers they are not likely to think of considerations or issues that make decisions and plans effective. Furthermore, perceptions of managers about the sources of their success are highly subjective, and the skills they cite are not a useful foundation for management or leadership standards.

One voice that has attempted to draw attention to decisions as fundamental to managerial effectiveness, is that of Herbert A. Simon. According to Simon, decisions are the key to effective managerial actions. (Simon, 1976). (It should be noted that Simon used the terms *administration* and *administrator* the way most writers use *management* and *manager*).

> *Administration* is ordinarily discussed as the art of "getting things done". Emphasis is placed upon processes and methods for insuring incisive action...it has not been commonly recognized that a theory of administration should be concerned with the processes of decisions as well as with the processes of action.

Still, Simon never listed the types of decisions that managers have to make, nor investigated the criteria that could be used to ensure their quality, such as the issues raised by the 8-Questions Model.

Research to Determine What Factors Bring Organizational Effectiveness

The record of management research is another source for gaining insight into what might bring continuing improvement—the key to high-level organizational effectiveness. There are many foundations from which business and non-business organizations have reached for this goal. They appear in the literature under various groupings such as: appropriate attention to both task and people factors (Blake & Srygley-Mouton, 1968), leadership practices in a more general sense (Kahn and Katz, 1960, Hersey & Blanchard, 1982, Vecchio, 1997, and others), many factors primarily related to business strategy (Peters & Austin, 1985; Peters & Waterman, 1982), effective reengineering (Hammer & Champy, 1993), effectiveness of teams (Katzenbach & Smith, 1993), attention to quality (Deming, 1986, Juran, 1989; Torbert 1992), outstanding service (various authors), benchmarking and emulation of best practices (various authors), and continuing learning (Senge, 1990).

All these foundations, of course, contribute to organizational performance. Following the approaches suggested by these viewpoints will, undoubtedly, help any organization achieve better results. The problem is that none of these potential foundations necessarily lead to high quality management and leadership in a comprehensive sense. None provide useful standards or criteria that, in turn, can serve to measure their impact.

Most of the foundations referred to above imply or suggest, in one way or another, that measurement can be based on the slippery ground of revenue, sales, or other financial comparisons. That, however, may fail to show the impact of external influences that are beyond the control of the decision makers. Some activities, and especially functions such as finance and accounting, information systems, production control and scheduling, even quality assurance and marketing when they are support functions, are not really measured by such an approach—they are covered by the broad brush of profitability and growth.

Two best-selling books, *In Search for Excellence* (Peters & Waterman, 1982) and *A Passion for Excellence* (Peters & Austin, 1985), whose titles sound as though they might shed light on what excellence is, fail to provide meaningful definitions that allow reasonable measurement of level of excellence, or progress toward it.

In Search for Excellence suggests eight attributes of excellent companies. They apparently are the titles of eight of the twelve titles in Part III of the book (apparently, because the book never lists them—it assumes that the reader will realize what they are). The eight titles are:

1. A bias for action
2. Close to the customer
3. Autonomy and entrepreneurship
4. Productivity through people
5. Hands-on, value-driven
6. Stick to the knitting
7. Simple form, lean staff, and
8. Simultaneous loose-tight properties

This is certainly a complicated list of items for which it would be most difficult to develop measurement criteria.

In *A Passion for Excellence*, the authors simplified the "standards". They reduced them to four elements. This time they stated them clearly.

"So, this is our model:

1. Care of customers
2. Constant innovation
3. Turned-on people
4. Yet one thing is missing, one element that connects all the others.... It is leadership. Leadership means vision, cheerleading, enthusiasm, love, trust, verve, passion, obsession, consistency, the use of symbols, paying attention as illustrated by the content of one's calendar, out-and-out drama (and the management thereof), creating heroes at all levels, coaching, effectively wandering around, and numerous other things."

It would not be an easy task to establish criteria for measuring the first three of these. But the fourth one—how could anyone get a handle on that one, the way it is described?

Having said all that about the need for standards makes it incumbent to suggest a definition of standards and criteria that could be used. Decision and plan quality could be such a standard. It may seem to be as difficult to measure as the level of management skills. As has been shown, that is not the case. There are abundant criteria in the literature for all decisions, the technical ones and those that are called leadership decisions here. All can be organized for use in measurement as is done with the 8-Questions Model (See Chapter 2).

With the sophistication of modern technology it is conceivable that measurement could include all significant decisions and plans. Or, a specific organization could limit it to the key results areas of productivity, quality of all aspects of product and/or service, staff competence, and staff member satisfaction. Depending on the type and needs of an organization, significant decisions and plans (those affecting the key results areas) of all staff members could be included, or only those in selected managerial and professional activities.

As briefly discussed in this chapter, gaining agreement on decision and plan quality is not difficult in those aspects that pertain to the "technical" fields. However in the issues that pertain to leadership-in-management, there is little awareness of what should be included. It is also likely that agreement would not be universal even if there were greater awareness. Not that widespread agreement on a comprehensive list of areas (managerial responsibilities), for which decisions and plan criteria are needed, is really necessary. It would seem that any organization could define the criteria in terms of managerial responsibilities in its own terms, and then ensure that it has set the standards for quality that allow it to measure performance against them. Still, to be most effective, defining the considerations, or questions to be used, is highly desirable.

There is one interesting idea pertaining to decision quality that deserves mention here. It is a negative but nonetheless valuable approach that alerts to common decision traps that should be avoided. Decision Traps are discussed in detail in Russo and Shoemaker (1989). The authors have identified 10 such traps:

1. Tendency to plunge in
2. Frame blindness
3. Lack of frame control
4. Overconfidence
5. Short-sightedness
6. Shooting from the hip
7. Group failure
8. Fooling yourself about feedback
9. Not keeping track
10. Failure to audit your decisions

Please note that all these apply equally to plans (groups of related decisions). The word "Frame" deserves clarification. The authors use the word to define the mental structures that people create to simplify and organize the world so that complexity is reduced. A frame thus helps to decide what information is needed, what alternatives can validly be considered, and how they could or should be evaluated.

Avoiding decision traps is, of course, important. To a limited extent the traps that Russo and Shoemaker describe in their book display some similarity to the 8-Question Model because they, too, lead to questions about various aspects of decisions. They do not, however, systematically raise issues pertaining to managerial or leadership responsibilities. As a complementary thought process that might be synergistic, keeping the traps in mind can be most beneficial.

Why Research Fails to Focus on Leadership Decisions

The failure of management theory to come to grips with the key issues of leadership decisions may be one reason why there is so little progress in research on management and leadership effectiveness. Other possible reasons are that higher-level managers believe they know all they need to know about decision making on management and leadership issues, and the parallel lack of interest in these issues in academia.

Still another reason may lie with the lure of the big decisions that are believed to be central to success, and certainly are so, at least for the short run. These concern the decisions in research, product, marketing and financial strategies, and in organizational structure. There is no doubt that decisions on reengineering, and restructuring all have far greater appeal to top management than the nitty gritty of helping the organization enhance decision making and planning competence at all levels, and in all management/leadership areas. This fascination with the 'big' decisions applies whether they involve decentralization or greater centralization, mergers and acquisitions, spin-offs and asset sales, downsizing, or changing the organizational layers, or even major new programs for the entire organizations such as TQM.

The rise and decline of blue chip companies such as Xerox, Lucent, Enron, Supermarkets General, Bradlees, Woolworth, and Grand Union, and the extensive, often preventable layoffs, continuously highlight the shallow approaches to decisions and plan. Competent planning and analyses of the situations at *all* levels, combined with effective two-way communications between managerial layers are likely to ameliorate, at least in part, these seemingly unnecessary sharp fluctuations and the organizational disruptions that follow in their wake. All that however requires, first of all, widespread competence in arriving at quality decisions and plans.

All this is not meant to suggest that there is no literature on decision-making. There just is nothing specifically applicable to issues to consider in leadership decisions, or even management decisions. Beyond the work of Simon

(1976), the bulk of what there is pertains to mathematical approaches generally considered in Operations Research, is geared toward psychological issues (Plous, 1993; Russo & Schoemaker, 1989), or is for the general public, including leaders and managers, of course. None of these provides comprehensive guidelines for leadership decisions, though some is indeed actionable and even universally applicable.

Focus on Issues to Consider in Decisions and Plans, As a Promising Approach

Why should emphasis be placed on decisions and plans, and the considerations that determine the quality of their outcomes? Because it is a topic that is of vast importance since decisions, and even plans, underlie all human behavior and actions, whether they lead to good or bad, to progress or retrogression.

Still, as pointed out before, there is the lack of attention to decisions, specific enough to allow useful standards for decision quality assessment. As Simon (1976) states: "Emphasis is placed upon processes and methods..." rather than on defining, developing, and assessing the quality of decisions. Though they lie at the core of the potential for high-level performance, decision and plan quality take backseats if they are considered at all. Most importantly, there is little in the way of a comprehensive approach to leadership decision and planning considerations.

Looking at decisions and plans as sources of actions can provide a foundation for a model that can supply practical guidelines for evaluation of progress toward the higher levels of performance quality.

A sound logical basis in the form of a conceptual model is clearly needed. If it is universally applicable, comprehensive, actionable and sufficiently specific, it can permit relatively objective evaluation of decision and plan quality along all relevant fields. A useful model can also help with improving decisions as they are made—in effect allowing real-time monitoring and evaluation of the decisions. When computerized, there is an audit trail that can help to fine-tune the model so that progress can accelerate. The management responsibilities and the criteria in the 8-Questions Model, to which they lead, are such a model. As the examples and the discussions in Chapters 3 and 13, and in the appendix to Chapter 11 show, use of the model improves all aspects of a decision or plan from determination of all the elements of the desirable outcome, to the selection and evaluation of the alternatives. It is also likely to point to consideration of short-term and long-term ancillary challenges that are not directly apparent in the situation, but which should nevertheless not be ignored.

REFERENCES

Adams, J. S. (1965). Inequity in social exchange. In L. Berkowitz (Ed.) *Advances in experimental social psychology. Vol. w:* 267–298. New York: Academy Press.

Alderfer, C. P. (May, 1969). A New Theory of Human Needs. *Organizational Behavior and Human Performance.*, 142–175.

Armstrong, M. (2000). *Performance management: key strategies and practical guidelines. Second edition.* London, UK: Kogan Page.

Avolio, B. J., & Bass, B. M. (1995). *You can drag a horse to water, but you can't make it drink: Evaluating a full range leadership model for training and development.* Unpublished paper, Center for Leadership Studies, Binghamton University, Binghampton, NY.

Bacal, R. (1998). *Performance management.* New York, NY: McGraw-Hill Trade.

Barnard, C. 1938. *Functions of the executive.* Cambridge MA: Harvard University Press.

Bennis, W., & Nanus, B. (1985) *Leadership: strategies for taking charge.* New York: Harper & Row.

Blake, R. R., & Srygley-Mouton, J. (1964). *The managerial grid.* Houston, TX: Gulf.

Blake, R. R., & Srygley-Mouton, J. (1968). *Corporate excellence through grid organization development.* Houston, TX: Gulf.

Blanchard, K. H., & Johnson, S. (1982). *The one-minute manager.* New York: Morrow.

Bramson, R. M. (1981). *Coping with difficult people.* Garden City, NY: Anchor Press.

Bruner, Jerome S. 1960. *The Process of Education.* Cambridge, MA: Harvard University Press.

Burns, J. M. (1978). *Leadership.* New York: Harper & Row.

Carter, H., & Rausch, E. (1999). *Management in the fire service (3rd ed.).* Quincy, MA: NFPA.

Conger, J. A., & Kanungo, R. A. (1987). *Charismatic leadership: The elusive in organizational effectiveness.* San Francisco, CA: Jossey-Bass.

Covey, S. R. (1989). *The seven habits of highly effective people: Restoring the character ethics.* New York: Simon & Schuster.

Covey, S. R. (1994). *First things first: To live, to love, to learn, to leave a legacy.* New York: Simon & Schuster.

Planning, Common Sense, and Superior Performance, pages 177–181

Cropanzano, R. (1993). *Justice in the workplace: Approaching fairness in human resource management.* Mahwah, NJ: Erlbaum.

Deci, E. I. (1975). *Intrinsic motivation.* New York: Plenum.

Deeprose, D. (1994). H*ow to recognize and reward employees.* NY: Amacom.

Deming, W. E. (1986). *Out of the crises.* Cambridge, MA: MIT Center for Advanced Engineering Study.

Didactic Systems. (1974). *Appraising employee performance: A self-study unit.* Cranford, NJ: Didactic Systems.

Didactic Systems. (1977a). *Managing and allocating time: A didactic simulation exercise.* Cranford, NJ: Didactic Systems.

Didactic Systems. (1977b). *Managing time effectively: A self-study unit.* Cranford, NJ: Didactic Systems.

Didactic Systems. (1977c). S*trategies for motivation: A self-study unit.* Cranford, NJ: Didactic Systems.

Didactic Systems, (1996). *Achievement stimulating process.* Cranford, NJ.

Fayol, H. (1949) G*eneral and industrial management.* (originally published in French, in 1916). New York: Pitman.

Fiedler, F. E. (1967). *A theory of leadership effectiveness.* New York: McGraw Hill.

Fisher, R., & Ury, W. (1981). *Getting to yes.* Boston: Houghton Mifflin.

Fleishman, E. A., Harris, E. F., & Burtt, R. D. (1955). *Leadership and supervision in industry* Columbus: Ohio State University Press.

Ghiselli, E. E. (1963). The validity of management traits in relation to occupational level. *Personnel Psychology, 16,* 109–113.

Golub, A. L. (1997). *Decision analysis: An integrated approach.* New York: Wiley.

Goodwin, P., & George W. (2004). *Decision analysis for management judgment. 3rd ed.* Hoboken, NJ: Wiley.

Graen, G., & Cashman, J. F. (1975). A role-making model of leadership in formal organizations: A developmental approach. In J. G. Hunt & L. L. Larson (Eds.), *Leadership frontiers* (pp. 143–165). Kent, OH: Kent State University Press.

Greenberg, J. (1993). The social side of fairness: Interpersonal and informational classes of organizational justice. In R. Cropanzano (Ed.), *Justice in the workplace: Approaching fairness in human resource management* (pp. 79–103). Mahwah, NJ: Erlbaum.

Hammer, M., & Champy, J. (1993). *Reengineering the corporation.* New York: Harper Business.

Heifetz, R. A., & Linsky, M. (2002). *Leadership on the line: Staying alive through the dangers of leading.* Boston: Harvard Business School Press.

Hersey, P., & Blanchard, K. H. (May, 1969). Life cycle theory of leadership. *Training and Development Journal. 23,* 2.

Hersey, P., & Blanchard, K. H. (1982). *Management of organizational behavior—Utilizing human resources. (4th ed.).* Englewood Cliffs, NJ: Prentice Hall.

Herzberg, F. (1968). One more time: How do you motivate employees? *Harvard Business Review. Jan/Feb.* No. 68108.

Herzberg, F., Mausner, B., & Snyderman, B. (1959). *The motivation to work.* New York: Wiley.

Hoch, S. J., Kunreuther, H. G., & Gunther, R. E. (Eds.) (2001). *Wharton on making decisions.* New York: Wiley.

House, R. J. (1971). A path-goal theory of leader effectiveness. *Administrative Science Quarterly, 16*(September), 321–338.

House, R. J., & Mitchell, T. R. (1974). Path–goal theory of leadership. *Journal of Contemporary Business,* Autumn, 81–97.

Hughes, C. L. (1965). *Goal setting—Key to individual and organizational effectiveness.* New York: American Management Association.

Juran, J. M. (1989). *Juran on leadership for quality: An executive handbook.* New York: The Free Press.

Kahn, R., & Katz, D. (1960). Leadership Practices in Relation ot Productivity and Morale. In D. Cartwright & A. Zander (Eds.) *Group dynamics, research and theory, 2nd ed.* Elmsford, NY: Row, Paterson.

Katzenbach, J. R., & Smith, D. K. (1993). *The wisdom of teams—Creating the high performance organization.* New York: Harper Business.

Kepner, C. H., & Tregoe, B. B. (1965). *The rational manager.* Princeton, NJ: Kepner-Tregoe.

Kepner, C. H., & Tregoe, B. B. (1981). *The new rational manager.* Princeton, NJ: Princeton Research Press.

Knowles, M. (1990). *The adult learner, a neglected species. (4th ed.)* Houston TX: Gulf.

Koontz, H. (1980). The management theory jungle revisited. *Academy of Management Review, 5*(2), 175–187.

Lakein, A. (1973). *How to get control of your time and your life.* New York: P.H. Wyden.

Latham, G. P., & Yukl, G. A. (1975). A review of research on the application of goal-setting in organizations. *Academy of Manamgement Journal,* December, 824–845.

Likert, R. (1961). *New patterns of management.* New York: McGraw-Hill.

Locke, E. A., & Latham, G. P. (1984). *Goal setting—A motivational technique that works.* Englewood Cliffs, NJ: Prentice Hall.

Locke, E. A., & Latham, G. P. (1990). *A theory of goal setting and task performance.* Englewood Cliffs, NJ: Prentice Hall.

Maier, N. R.F. (1967). Assets and liabilities in group problem solving: the need for an integrative function. *Psychological Review, 74*(4), 240–241.

Magoon, P. M., & Richards, J. B. (1966). *Discipline or disaster: Mmanagement's only choice; How to fulfill employees' basic emotional job-security needs.* New York: Exposition Press.

Martinko, M, (1995). *Attribution theory: An organizational perspective.* Boca Raton, FL: CRC Press.

Maslow, A. H. (1954). *Motivation and personality.* New York: Harper & Row.

Mayo, E. (1933, 1946). *The human problems of an industrial civilization.* Boston, MA: Harvard Business School.

McCauley, C. D., & Moxley, R. S. (1998). *The center for creative leadership handbook of leadership development.* Center for Creative Leadership.

McClelland, D. C. (1961). *The Achieving Society.* New York: Van Nostrand.

McElroy, J. C. (1982). A typology of attribution leadership research. *Academy of Management Journal. March,* 91–209.

McGregor, D. (1960). *The human side of enterprise.* New York: McGraw-Hill.

Moorhead, G., & Griffin, R. W. (1992). *Organizational behavior: Managing people and organizations, (3rd ed.).* Boston: Houghton Mifflin.

Nelson, B. (1994). *1001 ways to reward employees.* New York: Workman.

Nelson, B. (1997). *1001 ways to energize employees.* New York: Workman.

Nutt, P. C. (2002). *Why decisions fail: Avoiding the blunders and traps that lead to debacles.* Williston, VT: Berrett-Koehler.

Odiorne, G. S. (1968). *Management decisions by objectives.* Englewood Cliffs, NJ: Prentice-Hall.

Peters, T., & Austin, N. (1985). *A passion for excellence: The leadership difference.* New York: Random House.

Peters, T., & Waterman, R. H. Jr. (1982). *In search of excellence: Lessons from America's best-run companies.* New York: Harper & Row.

Plous, S. (1993). *The psychology of judgment and decision making.* New York: McGraw-Hill.

Plunkett, W. R., & Attner, R. F. (1992). *Introduction to management (4th ed.)* Wadsworth.

Rausch, E. (1978/1985). *Balancing needs of people and organizations—The linking elements concept.* Washington, DC: Bureau of National Affairs (1978). Cranford, NJ: Didactic Systems.

Rausch, E. (Ed.). (1980). *Management in institutions of higher learning.* Lexington, MA: Lexington Books.

Rausch, E. (1985). *Win-win performance management/appraisal.* New York: Wiley.

Rausch, E. (July/August, 1996). Challenge: Performance evaluations, *The TQM Magazine. 8*(4), 71–72.

Rausch, E., & Rausch, G. (1971). *Leading groups to better decisions: A business game.* Cranford, NJ: Didactic Systems.

Rausch, E., Sherman, H., & Washbush, J. B. (2003). Defining and assessing competencies for competency-based, outcome-focused management development. *Journal of Management Development, 21*(3), 184–200.

Rausch, E., & Washbush, J. B. (1998). *High quality leadership: practical guidelines to becoming a more effective manager.* Milwaukee, WI: Quality Press.

Rausch, E., & Wohlking, W. (1969). *Handling conflict in management I,III and III—Business games.* Cranford, NJ: Didactic Systems.

Robbins, S. P. (1991). *Management, 3rd ed.* Englewood Cliffs, NJ: Prentice Hall.

Russo, E. J., & Schoemaker, P. J. H. (1989). *Decision traps: Ten barriers to brilliant decision-making and how to overcome them.* Fireside Books.

Russo, E. J., & Schoemaker, P. J. H. (2002). *Winning decisions.* New Yok: Doubleday.

Senge, P. M. (1990}. *The fifth discipline—The art and practice of the learning organization.* New York: Currency and Doubleday.

Simon, H. A. (1976). *Administrative behavior: A study of decision making processes in administrative organizations.* New York: The Free Press.

Skinner, B. F. (1968). *The technology of teaching.* New York: Appleton Century Crofts.

Steers, R. M., & Porter, L. W. (1979). M*otivation and work behavior, 2nd ed.* New York: McGraw-Hill.

Stogdill, R. M. (1974). *Handbook of leadership: A survey of theory and research.* New York: Free Press.

Tannenbaum, R., & Schmidt, W. H. (1958). How to choose a leadership pattern. *Harvard Business Review.* March/ April, 96 (revisited May/June 1973).

Taylor, F. W. (1911). *The principles of scientific management.* New York: W.W. Norton & Co.

Torbert, W. (1992) The true challenge of generating continual quality improvement. *Journal of Management Inquiry, 1*(4), 331–336.

Ury, W. (1991). *Getting past no.* New York: Bantam Books.

Vecchio, R. P. (1997). Situational Leadership Theory: An Examination of a Prescriptive Theory. In Vecchio (Ed.), *Leadership: understanding the dynamics of power and influence in organizations.* South Bend, IN: University of Notre Dame Press.

Vroom, V., & Jago, A. G. (1988). *Managing participation in organizations.* Englewood Cliffs, NJ: Prentice Hall.

Vroom, V., & Yetton, P. W. (1973). *Leadership and decision-making.* Pittsburgh: University of Pittsburgh Press.

Whetten, D. A., & Cameron, K. S. (1993). *Developing management skills: Managing conflict.* New York: HarperCollins.

Whetten, D. A., & Cameron, K. S. (1995). *Developing management skills, 3rd.ed.* New York: HarperCollins.

Wright, G. (Ed.) (1985). *Behavioral decision making.* New York: Plenum Press.

Yukl, G. A. (1981). *Leadership in organizations.* Englewood Cliffs, NJ: Prentice Hall.

APPENDIX

A FEW MORE WORDS ABOUT THIS BOOK

Like most books, this one has a long history. In fact it has three—one for the concepts, which gives it a foundation that is based solidly on the literature pertaining to management, leadership, interpersonal relations, and learning. A second history can be told about the system of successively more specific issues raised by questions and subsidiary questions which provide a bridge between theory and practice. A third one could document the travails of the author. There are relevant poems which summarize them. The poem for the first two is in Part II of Alexander Pope's Essay on Criticism:

A little learning is a dangerous thing;
Drink deep, or taste not the Pierian spring:
There shallow draughts intoxicate the brain,
And drinking largely sobers us again.
Fired at first sight at what the Muse imparts,
In fearless youth we tempt the heights of Arts,
While from the bounded level of our mind,
Short views we take, nor see the lengths behind;
But more advanced, behold with strange surprise
New distant scenes of endless science rise!

The third one can be summed up more succinctly with a few lines, slightly modified, from another famous poem:

First across the gulf we cast, Kite born threads, till lines are passed
And then, habit builds the bridge, at last.
—John B. O'Reilly, *A Builder's Lesson*

Planning, Common Sense, and Superior Performance, pages 183–197

Suffice it to say that much of the theoretical foundations can be found in *Balancing Needs of People and Organizations: The Linking Elements Concept*, a book on the 3Cs model of management, which I wrote with great expectations, in the late 1970s. It was good to us (not the royal "us" or the first person plural, but those of us in the company and some external consultants, who reaped the benefits); several large organizations built their management development programs on it and it sold a satisfactory number of copies. It did not, however, meet our expectations. An attempt to gain broader attention which also fell short of expectations is in Erwin Rausch and John B. Washbush, 1998, *High Quality Leadership: Practical Guidelines to Becoming a More Effective Manager*, ASQ Quality Press, Milwaukee, WI. Both books, and especially the second one can be most useful in providing broader perspective, alternate approaches, and greater detail on the issues discussed here. They will, undoubtedly serve even better for some readers who are more inclined to prefer the respective structures they provide.

This book, I hope, is even more reader friendly, though it does not contain as many scenarios as its predecessor, because it covers the concepts from an easier-to-follow perspective. Like the previous books, it presents views about leadership and also for practicing leadership.

Especially for the benefit of readers who are knowledgeable in what the academic world refers to as Organizational Behavior, it is important to point out that this book does not bring any new formal research results. In fact, there is little that is 'new' in the way of theory. The strength of this book lies in the way it shapes conclusions, from practical experience, past research and existing theories, into a realistic, detailed model.

To avoid false modesty, I am, however, listing the significant conceptual contributions that provide foundations for segments of this book, and in different ways for the previous ones. They are:

- The comprehensive list of questions which managers should take into account when dealing with the issues they face
- The emphasis on the two separate aspects of every managerial decision and plan—the functional (technical) and the management/leadership considerations. (Rausch & Washbush, 1998)
- The introduction of a third consideration in every decision—attention to the process of decision making and planning, including the steps in the process, possibly the use of decision support systems, and consideration/awareness of psychological influences such as personal values and attitudes toward risk
- The distinction between goals and action steps, which can have great impact on the outcomes of management/leadership actions (Rausch, 1978/85).
- The application of the distinction between importance and urgency to goal selection and priority setting which was previously published

in various titles on time management and others (Didactic Systems, 1977a, 1977b; Rausch 1978, 1985). Stephen Covey has since made the concept famous in *The Seven Habits of Highly Effective People* (1989) and in *First Things First* (1994), possibly without awareness of our prior publications that had only relatively limited distribution.

- The separation of needs, in Maslow's Hierarchy, into those which can be satisfied with psychological rewards and those which require tangible rewards (Didactic Systems 1977c; Rausch, 1978/1985). This distinction emphasizes the great many ways in which managers/leaders can show appreciation for contributions of staff members, the steady but mundane, as well as the outstanding ones.

Three less significant contributions by the author may also deserve brief mention here:

- The definition of *fairness* in performance appraisal (Rausch, 1985).
- The idea that all parties in a conflict can appoint themselves to be 'Managers of Conflict' and thereby contribute more effectively to its resolution. (Rausch & Washbush, 1998)
- The importance of using a wide range of approaches for showing appreciation for steady non-spectacular contributions by staff members, not only for those that are outstanding. (Didactic Systems, 1996)

Differential definitions of management and leadership have deliberately been avoided. All definitions of these terms are highly subjective (Stogdill, 1974; Bennis & Nanus, 1985) and it seems best to stay away from the many controversies that swirl around them.

The ideas expressed in this book have proven their worth in many hundreds of cases. Managers, in various private and public management development programs were asked to use them for reviewing decisions or plans. Almost without exception, all managers made some change, sometimes small ones, sometimes significant ones, in their previous decisions or plans, after considering just a short summary list of questions.

If you apply the Eight-Questions Model suggested here to one or two of your decisions or plans, they will stimulate you to dig deeper. Then you will know more about the concepts on which they are founded and be able to apply them with greater confidence, and to more complex situations. Keep in mind, however, that the groups of issues, as offered here, are not a final word. You are encouraged to modify the list or the wording so they fit well into the way you make decisions and develop plans.

Beyond serving as quality checks for decisions and plans before they are implemented, a list of issues to consider in decisions can also provide structure and focus for preparing reports and proposals to management. They help to ensure that all bases are touched.

VALIDATION QUESTIONS

As mentioned in Chapter 1, on conceptual foundation, neither the Eight-Questions Model nor the previous explanations of the same decision-and-plan-guiding concept, as it was reflected in the basic and comprehensive 3Cs diagram, has found widespread acceptance in the literature (though it has been used widely). Critical and knowledgeable readers have therefore raised questions about validity. They pertain primarily to the origin of the concept and to any support (either empirical or in the literature) that can serve to validate it. Chapter 1 was not an appropriate place to respond to these questions. They are therefore discussed below.

Question: What support is there for the concept behind the Eight-Questions Model?

Support is of two kinds—literature foundations and undocumented use.

a. Literature Foundations

As indicated previously, literature foundation for the *participation* question can be found in the insights offered by Tannenbaum and Schmidt (1958/73), Maier(1967), Fiedler (1967), Hersey and Blanchard (1969 and 1982), and others. Outstanding work on this issue has been and continues to be done by Victor Vroom and his associates (Vroom & Yetton, 1973; Vroom & Jago, 1988). The collaborators have worked on this challenge for years and have made considerable progress. In a similar vein, (House & Terence, 1974; Hughes, 1965; Latham & Yukl, 1975; Locke & Latham, 1990; Odiorne, 1968; Rausch, 1978/85, 1980, 2002; Yukl, 1998), and others, have independently developed some more or less specific criteria that can help to bring sound decisions pertaining to the effective use of *goals* (objectives) in an organization. With respect to *satisfaction* there is the rich literature on motivations stemming from, and expanding on Mayo's Hawthorne experiments, from Maslow's hierarchy of needs (Maslow 1954), and Herzberg's motivation/hygiene theory (Herzberg. 1959, 1968) and more recently, Nelson (1994).[1]

1. There are readers who may feel that the citations in these paragraphs are too dated to be of full value and that more recent writing should have been cited. The answer to this concern is that, what has been quoted, are the foundation writing on these topics. There does not appear to be anything in later literature that adds significant value to the concepts. However, should something emerge, it is highly unlikely that it will affect the Eight-Questions model, since it would automatically become part of the subsidiary information and foundation for the respective question.

On other fronts, there are vast literature resources that bring foundation for decisions aand strategies pertaining competence development, specifically in books and papers on processes, techniques, and conditions for learning, and learning styles. The same is true for communications, for norms related to work, ethics, and biases, for coordination and cooperation, and for appropriate performance evaluation based on regular performance/progress reviews.

b. Undocumented Use

The Eight-Questions concept has developed first from the author's experience as practicing manager at a high level in two companies with about 500 employees, and then from more than three decades of learning needs analyses during design and conduct of management development programs, including simulations, writing of articles and books on the leadership aspect of management, editing special issues of journals on leadership, teaching of leadership in management courses at the graduate level, and many years of designing and testing simulation games on practically all management functions.

At first, Didactic Systems' staff provided the responses to attendee/participant decisions in simulation designs for human resource development programs. These were based on staff views and were then revised as necessary during pilot use. Dissatisfaction with such haphazard, mainly subjective responses led to a search for a universally applicable, comprehensive and actionable model that was supported by the research reported on in the literature. The foundation concept, based on manager and leader responsibilities that emerged from that search has been presented in different but similar models, without any substantive challenges, contradictions, and change, in 25 years of use. That use has been in human resource programs for the entire Federal Prison System, the training arms of the US Office of Personnel and the Alberta Government, continuing use in fire departments in many states, JCPenney, the Girl Scouts, several hospitals, seminars of the American Management Associations, and many other lesser programs for business organizations such as Schering-Plough, and U.S. Air. It has been depicted in the West Point Academy book on leadership, in Heyel's Encyclopedia of Management and in General Electric's summary handout to management learners at all levels.

Still, there are undoubtedly questions other than the eight presented here, that could serve the same purpose, provided they are also universally applicable, equally integrated, comprehensive, specific and actionable, and supported by more detailed questions based on the literature, that lead the user closer to the most desirable aspects of the decision and plan alternative under consideration. However, in light of the literature support it seems undeniable that definition of desired outcome (in effect the thinking about goals), appropriate participation and communications, thought about necessary competencies, and satisfaction of stakeholders, would have to be components of any set of questions to ask when making decisions.

There is no specific empirical evidence of the Eight-Question Model's effectiveness in bringing "better management or leadership" except as extension of the research reported on in the literature. Validating the enormously complex concept would take generations and huge financial resources, in light of the many uncontrollable factors. That is demonstrated by the many years that Victor Vroom and his associates have worked on a still incomplete set of guidelines for selection of only participation level.

The decision-and-plan-guiding concept in the 3Cs and in the Eight-Question Model thus evolved simultaneously from literature review and from the extensive use of segments in simulation game trials, with subjective validation based on the views of literally thousands of managers. Throughout the many years, since before 1978 when the first book was published, not one substantive objection or contradiction has been raised. There was one thought that was not in the original model, but has since been added. It concerned the role of values and ethics in norms.

Question: What support is there to validate the flexibility of the model and its adaptability to other cultures?

Seminar attendees and graduate students from many regions of the world, including European, Indian, Pacific Rim, and South American countries, have confirmed that the model adapts to other cultures.

However, logic can also confirm this universal applicability. If one actually applies any of the eight questions, and their subsidiary ones, to an issue, it becomes apparent that it is the orientation of the decision-maker-planner that shapes the answers. A US manager's answer to the participation questions is likely to be more democratic than the answer of a South American. Still, the answer would be equally valid because it would be appropriate to the environment and relationships.

The model automatically adjusts to new research findings because such new findings would become part of the background information behind the respective question—or possibly add another question to the list of questions that the decision-maker uses. The addition of values and ethics to the question on norms, incidentally, attests to the flexibility of the model and the ease with which it can adapt to new inputs.

One more thought. In light of the flexibility of the model, if a substantive objection were to arise, its point could undoubtedly be incorporated, either as an adjustment of one of the eight questions, or possibly even as a ninth question.

SHOWING APPRECIATION

The immediate effect of a show of appreciations is a fleeting pleasant moment for at least one staff member. Pleasant moments can have "contagious" effects, reinforcing each other throughout an organization, creating a constantly strengthening positive climate. They are like smiles:

A smile is quite a funny thing. It wrinkles up your face,
And when it's gone, you'll never find its secret hiding place.
But far more wonderful it is to see what smiles can do;
You smile at one, he smiles at you,
And so one smile makes two.
Now, since a smile can do great good
By cheering hearts of care,
Let's smile and smile, and not forget
That smiles go everywhere!
—Unknown

There are many likely overtones to the multiplying effects that develop when staff members know that their manager appreciates their contributions:

- Staff members are more likely to feel good about their work, and they are then challenged to do at least as well in the future. They will want to continue to deserve high regard, and any extra attention to their work that they may contribute is hardly felt because the sign of appreciation has made the work a little more pleasant.
- Staff members feel more confident in coming forward with suggestions. Action on these suggestions further strengthens the positive bond between staff member and manager, while bringing a direct benefit in effectiveness, quality, safety, or customer relations.
- Staff members develop better understanding of the manager's views, and are more comfortable and secure as a result of increased trust.
- When the manager involves other departments by extending the signs of appreciation to the members of these other departments, inter-departmental conflicts are less likely. Reciprocating actions by managers and members of other departments add further positive moments.
- Sometimes, managers can involve clients, customers, patient family members, or other 'outsiders' with similar results in improved relations.

Even when the climate is healthy, these actions gradually lead to even better mutual understanding between managers and other staff members and the bonds strengthen.

These benefits are not likely to come immediately when you show more frequent signs of appreciation. They will surely come, however, if you are sincere, sharpen your skills for recognizing the wide range of performance and personality strengths, make full use of the many ways to show appreciation, and persevere.

There is one other benefit of no-cost signs of appreciation: it is unlikely that unions and other employee organizations will object to them, as they may do when they believe that an incentive awards program is an effort by the organization to get staff members to work harder, and produce more.

Noticing Achievements

Anybody can notice outstanding, unusual contribution. Managers rarely have a tough time identifying the best performers in any activity and let those staff member know (at least once in a while) that they consider them tops in that respect. What about the second best, or even the third best? What if they are all good, even though not as good as the best? How likely is it that managers will notice them and show some outward signs that they appreciate the contributions?

Managers need to identify the areas where each staff member's unique contributions are.

The list in *Types of Achievements,* below gives examples of the types of specific achievements, activities and staff member characteristics that are helpful and deserve acknowledgement. It includes suggestions for only very few occupations and is by no means complete. There is also considerable overlap. You should be able to prune and extend it to make it appropriate for your people. Moreover, during any one time period, you can emphasize those items on the list which focus on one or more activities that you want to stress such as for example: quality, safety, attendance, or customer relations.

You can use the list as a starter. Better yet, spend a few minutes every day, thinking about things that your staff had done the day before. You'll be surprised to see how the list will keep growing, and also become more specific. You might start with the obvious: quantity and quality of work, working longer hours, not spending extra time on breaks, regular attendance, meeting deadlines, skill in handling non-routine assignments, maintaining appropriate work-area appearance, participating constructively in meetings, following procedures, courtesy and calmness when speaking with clients, willingness to learn new routines or tasks, etc.

You would then become more sensitive to staff member behavior that is not as directly related to overall responsibilities and the tasks at hand, but rather contributes in different ways—not letting conflicts erupt but settling them, helping to maintain a friendly and cheerful atmosphere, assisting others who had questions or difficulties with a task, especially when a new program was introduced, maintaining non-routine records, finding things that had been misplaced. Once you are serious about expanding your list, it probably will never end.

Types of Achievements

Activities Applicable to Most Work Environments Include:

- Planning
- Meeting deadlines
- Safety and use of safe practices
- Quantity of work
- Accuracy and quality of work
- Suggestions to improve the way the work is done
- Skill in handling stressful situations
- Skill in handling routine tasks and non-routine assignments
- Avoidance of waste and spoilage
- Activities involved in housekeeping and maintaining appropriate work-area appearance
- Caring for equipment
- Use of space
- Accuracy in record keeping
- Factualness and accuracy in communicating information

Administrative and Secretarial Activities

- Greeting customers, identifying their interests and needs, politeness, appropriateness of suggestions
- Typing, filing, transmitting messages, scheduling meetings, keeping logs and records
- Competent telephone communications

Financial and Information Systems Activities

- Recording, arranging and analyzing data
- Activities related to budgets, financial and data recording systems
- Modifying, or recommending a modification in a system
- Preparation of reports
- Computer programming and troubleshooting
- Use of equipment and materials
- Use of techniques, and methods

- Handling customer/client complaints
- Administrative activities
- Budget development and implementation

Research and Development Activities

- Design of experiments and studies
- Collecting, recording and analyzing data
- Use of equipment and materials
- Budget development and implementation
- Preparation of reports and papers

Activities in Interpersonal Relations

- Cooperation and teamwork
- Assisting others
- Verbal expression
- Effective use of questions
- Presentation before a group
- Serving as a role model
- Listening
- Contributing at meetings
- Conduct in controversies
- Written communications (memos, letters, proposals)
- Using humor effectively

Personal Characteristics

- Attendance and punctuality
- Reliability in achieving results
- Being available
- Meeting commitments
- Sound decision making
- High personal standards (quality, quantity, reliability, dependability)
- Cheerfulness
- Creativity, innovation and imagination
- Incisiveness
- Acceptance of and ability to cope with pressure
- Empathy
- Helping to prevent and resolve conflict
- Helping to ensure open communications
- Showing the positive when others show dissatisfactions

Showing Appreciation for Staff Member Contributions and Accomplishments With Psychological Rewards (Intangibles)

That's the hardest part for most managers/leaders. Most are good at saying "thanks," paying personal compliments, talking about family matters, and joking about sports. They can say "that's great" when a staff member reports some accomplishment that is pleasant to hear, that is needed for some project, or that they sense the staff member is proud of.

In a more significant vein, some managers show their high regard for the members of their teams in a variety of ways: by taking their suggestions seriously, by asking for their opinions, and by consulting with them on many decisions. Whenever possible, these managers will share information they obtain about what is going on inside and outside the organization.

By blurring the distinctions between the job of the manager and the jobs of the other team members, competent managers create a highly positive climate in which each member of the team can feel secure and wanted.

Still, most managers neglect the opportunity to enrich the workday for their people by regularly showing evidence of their appreciation for the positive things the members of their team contribute.

There are many specific ways for bringing rewarding moments to staff members, for saying thanks, at several levels of seriousness and emphasis. At one extreme is simply saying "thank you" for a task the staff member completed, possibly with different words like "that (task accomplished or beneficial action) is great." A pleased expression, a friendly wave of the hand, or even a pat on the arm or shoulder, a high-five, or a handshake (if it comes naturally), when added to the words, raises the level of the gesture.

Paying compliments about appearance, talking about family matters, sports, TV or social events are similar, yet less relevant ways of showing that the staff members' contributions are appreciated.

For a clearer view of what staff members expect in the way of appreciation can be found when listening to what people say. There is widespread agreement among staff members in all types of organizations on what would make them feel good about going to work every morning, to a job where the day flies by quickly, and where they would prefer to finish what they are doing rather than leave on time. See Question 5.3 for fundamental ways to show appreciation.

The list below recognizes the common needs as demonstrated by seminar participants and provides the seeds for many basic ways to show appreciation in non-tangible ways. The first items are relatively mild and the last are the strongest. The list is not exhaustive, nor are the items mutually exclusive; most can be used in conjunction with one or more of the others. More important, there are no unique items in the list. You have undoubtedly used every one, either frequently or on occasion. The purpose in providing the list is to supply a reference and a starter. It should stimulate ideas for expanding it and make it easier for you to use these simple means of showing appreciation more frequently, and possibly more consistently.

Verbal expressions of appreciation (either spoken or informal notes):

- Pointing to the importance of a *specific* accomplishment
- Indicating awareness of a *specific* accomplishment that came to your attention without the staff member's knowledge
- Offering help with an assignment
- Asking for an explanation of how a difficult task was accomplished
- Distinguishing the 'thanks' from routine acknowledgements by setting them deliberately into a different place or time, such as your office, in front of other staff members from your and/or other department(s) informally, or even formally, etc.
- Asking for ideas and suggestions
- Asking for the staff member's opinion on one of your ideas or of ideas and suggestions from others
- Promptly providing information on occurrences affecting the team
- Arranging for members, or the manager, of another department to provide any of the items above
- Arranging for a higher level manager to provide any of the items above
- Arranging, through verbal or written requests, for customers or members of the public with whom an staff member may be in regular contact, to provide any of the items above
- Including a staff member in the list of those to whom management/leadership tasks (that the staff member can perform) are delegated such as leading a meeting in your absence, or taking your place at an inter-departmental meeting which you cannot attend
- Initiating career counseling and responding effectively to questions on career opportunities
- Giving full consideration to staff members during the selection of candidates for vacant positions
- Helping staff members acquire skills that might be useful for positions up the career ladder (through developmental assignments or a training program)
- Taking the staff member into your 'confidence' on an event or a decision not yet public knowledge
- Promptly implementing a suggestion or idea
- Consulting regularly with a staff member who has the knowledge or experience to contribute effectively

These techniques blur the line between the work of the manager and the functions of other team members. They create a highly positive work climate that adds many pleasant moments to the work-day for team members and for the manager.

As pointed out in Providing Semi-Tangible Signs of Appreciation of Chapter 7, you have full control over non-tangible signs of appreciation that come from you. You also have considerable control over those that come from higher level managers since they are not likely to refuse a request from you to say something positive to one or several members of your team.

Help from other departments should also not be difficult to obtain, especially if you are willing to reciprocate. All it might take is for you and for some members of your team to show appreciation for achievements of members of the other departments, when these accomplishments favorably impact your team. If you want to be even more certain of cooperation, you can reach an informal agreement with the manager of the other department.

Gaining help from customers and/or other members of the public is not as easy, of course, but it can sometimes be stimulated, especially when your staff member has performed a service that is appreciated by the person. You can directly ask that person to send a note, thanking the staff member. Word can also go out that says, in effect: "When something is not what you expected, let me know; when everything is OK, let the person know with whom you have been in contact." If sent frequently, a message like this might bring some results.

Manager Concerns About Showing Appreciation

There are at least five reasons why so little attention is paid to this important need:

- Managers are not aware of the many benefits such attention could bring.
- Their organizations don't provide the necessary support.
- Managers are concerned that they might be perceived as showing favoritism if they then fail to show appreciation for someone else's contribution
- Managers think that they don't have the time.
- Managers haven't developed the skills and habits needed to show appreciation for many of the valuable contributions by team members.

Let's look at these reasons more closely.

The Benefits

As has been pointed out before, the benefits of showing appreciation can be really significant, both in their immediate and delayed effects. Some of the benefits may not come immediately when a manager begins to show more frequent signs of appreciation. They will surely come if the manager is sincere, develops skills for recognizing the wide range of performance and personality strengths, makes full use of the many ways to show appreciation, and perseveres.

Organizational Support

Organizational support can certainly make it easier to provide meaningful recognition. Still, strong, competent managers can accomplish much, even without organizational support, by making effective use of the many psychological awards that are always available. But they cannot do nearly as much alone as they can do with upper management's backing.

When the entire organization is actively involved, top management commitment and full endorsement, intensify the value of the recognition. Equally, or possibly more important, it supplies funds for tangible awards, which managers can use, in addition to the psychological ones. Organization support also furthers uniform actions in all departments.

Concern About Showing Favoritism

This concern, though possibly valid, is not a good reason for showing less appreciation for contributions than could be shown. If you show appreciation regularly and sincerely, staff members will give you credit for the effort and are not likely to quibble with what they realize may be unfair perceptions of favoritism. Benefits greatly outweigh this possible minor dissatisfaction by one or several individuals. As with most of your actions, it's the batting average that counts.

Not Enough Time for this Additional Responsibility

Even if providing signs of appreciation were an additional responsibility and were to require additional time, the benefits would make such time highly productive. That this activity needs significant chunks of time, however, is mainly a misconception. Award meetings are not the important issue—chances are that they take place already. If they don't, and time is really too tight, they won't be missed much if a manager effectively uses other approaches. Saying something pleasant about the work takes hardly any time. Even short hand-written notes take very little time. These two, however, are where "the tire meets the road"—this is where the beneficial action is.

Inadequate Skills and Habits

There may be a small investment of time to get started, but thereafter the sharpening of the two skills, and the development of the desirable habits—identifying contributions, and using many different ways to show appreciation—come naturally.

Printed in the United States
106886LV00001B/45/P

9 781593 118785